T2-CRY-155

STILL STANDING

James Merritt

HARVEST HOUSE PUBLISHERS
EUGENE, OREGON

Unless otherwise indicated, all Scripture quotations are from The Holy Bible, New International Version®, NIV®. Copyright © 1973, 1978, 1984, 2011 by Biblica, Inc.™ Used by permission of Zondervan. All rights reserved worldwide.

Verses marked ESV are from The Holy Bible, English Standard Version, copyright © 2001 by Crossway Bibles, a division of Good News Publishers. Used by permission. All rights reserved.

Verses marked NKJV are from the New King James Version. Copyright © 1982 by Thomas Nelson, Inc. Used by permission. All rights reserved.

Cover design by Koechel Peterson & Associates, Inc., Minneapolis, Minnesota

Cover photo © Stockbyte/Thinkstock

Published in association with the literary agency of Wolgemuth & Associates. Inc.

STILL STANDING
Copyright © 2012 by James Merritt
Published by Harvest House Publishers
Eugene, Oregon 97402
www.harvesthousepublishers.com

Library of Congress Cataloging-in-Publication Data

Merritt, James Gregory, 1952–
    Still standing / James Merritt.
        p. cm.
    ISBN 978-0-7369-4338-3 (pbk.)
    ISBN 978-0-7369-4339-0 (eBook)
    1. Christian life.   2. Suffering—Religious aspects—Christianity.   I. Title.
    BV4501.3.M4825   2012
    248.4—dc23
                                                            2012013488

All rights reserved. No part of this publication may be reproduced, stored in a retrieval system, or transmitted in any form or by any means—electronic, mechanical, digital, photocopy, recording, or any other—except for brief quotations in printed reviews, without the prior permission of the publisher.

Printed in the United States of America

12 13 14 15 16 17 18 19 20 / LB-KBD / 10 9 8 7 6 5 4 3 2 1

To Joanne Wardell and Kalli Overcash,
two magnificent assistants who helped me stand tall many days
when it would have been easier
to sit down, sleep in, step aside, or slip away.

Contents

1. When Life Knocks You Down 7

2. When Life Is Physically Draining 21
   Winning Strategy 1: Find Others to Stand with You

3. When Life Is Dragging You Down 35
   Winning Strategy 2: Stand Aside and Take a Break

4. When Life Is Unfair 51
   Winning Strategy 3: Remember That You Do Not Stand Alone

5. When Life Seems Impossible 69
   Winning Strategy 4: Stand on the Truth of God's Word

6. When Life Tempts You to Sell Out 83
   Winning Strategy 5: Make Sure You Stand Facing in the
   Right Direction

7. When Life Says "Run" 99
   Winning Strategy 6: Remember that the Cost of Standing Is
   Less than the Price of Surrendering

8. When Life Seems to Be Against You 115
   Winning Strategy 7: Stand Focused on the Task at Hand

9. When Life Is Insufferable 131
   Winning Strategy 8: Stand Under the Shadow of
   God's Strength

   Afterword: The Monday Morning Challenge
   to Remain Standing 147

   Notes 153

   Acknowledgments 157

1

When Life Knocks You Down

*"He knows not his own
strength who hath not met adversity."*

WILLIAM SAMUEL JOHNSON

The only time I'd seen the state of Mississippi was when I drove through it en route to Texas. All I remember was the balmy air. And mosquitoes. Lots of mosquitoes. Having only this one experience with the Magnolia State, I had no desire to visit again, much less live there. But as the saying goes, God has quite the sense of humor.

After graduating from seminary, I was called to pastor a country church in a sleepy Mississippi town called Laurel. Though it was the Jones County seat, it felt more like Mayberry. A small shopping district on Main Street. Houses lining residential areas with screened-in front porches and the occasional pink flamingo.

Unlike Mayberry, Laurel had a touch of mischief in her blood. Jones County is famous in those parts for one reason: It seceded from the Confederacy. That's right. Shortly after the Civil War began, the residents of Jones County thought they were better off by themselves, and they soon became known as "The Free State of Jones." I soon learned this would tell me all I needed to know about the independent thinking of the people of Jones County, but that's another story.

My wife and first two sons spent more than twenty-eight mostly fruitful ministry months there, but as the late Ray Charles said it, I always had Georgia on my mind. I pleaded with the Lord for an opportunity to pastor a church in my home state. Atlanta was only fifty miles from where I grew up and was a big city. Surely God could find a vacancy for me there.

In His sovereign grace, God opened a door. I packed up and drove my two sons and wife, who was now carrying our third child, to a suburb not far from Georgia's capital city. My task: to lead a sleeping giant of a church that was bursting with growth potential and ready to explode.

And explode it did. In ways I'd neither expected nor hoped for.

Hear Me Roar, Watch Me Wither

My first six months of ministry in our new church appeared to be a roaring success. Before I had arrived, the church had struggled to baptize fifty people in a single year and had endured financial struggles. We'd baptized a hundred new converts in my first ninety days, and suddenly found our bank balance in the black. Scores of new attendees flooded through our doors, and many members were added. But all was not well beneath the surface.

I had inherited a church where much of the ministerial staff did not share my theological convictions and ministerial philosophy. They opposed my coming from the beginning and led a concerted effort to keep the church from calling me. They also had poisoned the well with much of the lay leadership, and together the two groups made a combustible concoction that was bound to erupt. And with the power of Mount Vesuvius, it did.

My family began receiving nasty anonymous letters. Some members would give us cold stares after church. Others refused to speak to us. My wife seemed to bear the brunt of it. She was starved for friendship, but many women avoided her as if she had a communicable disease.

The resistance of cantankerous members was only matched by my mutinous staff. I'll never forget my first staff meeting. Even though it was a warm October day, the meeting room felt like a meat locker in a butcher's shop. Icicles formed on the windows, and I could see my breath. The staff assembled one by one as if they were going to hear the results of an oncology report. From the scowls on their faces, it was clear there would be no honeymoon.

I faced constant questioning of even routine decisions and was often ignored when I asked questions. They opposed any leadership I attempted to give and any changes I suggested, even if they were obviously needed.

Staff accountability? No luck. Whatever accountability I tried to build into the staff was met with fierce resistance. I actually sat with one staff member to politely but firmly ask him if he would (a) quit smoking at church, (b) quit using foul language, and (c) come to even one of the two worship services on Sunday mornings. I would have fired him if I could, but I had agreed to give the staff at least six months to see if we could work together. Big mistake.

My third son was born just three months after our arrival. It was the day after Christmas, and the only staff person who came to the hospital was the worship leader. He was one of the two ringleaders spearheading the opposition against me. He stayed perhaps two minutes, never even said a prayer, and smiled only once—when he turned to leave.

With my exhausted wife staring into my eyes, I knew my dream church had taken on nightmare qualities. We expected to saunter into this new phase of life standing tall, but without warning, life had knocked us down. And now it seemed to be kicking us.

When it became obvious that I could neither be intimidated nor deterred in giving the strong leadership the church needed, they turned up the heat. The platform I preached from was small and narrow, forcing me to preach only a couple of feet from the choir. As I preached, I'd hear choir members behind me whispering just loud enough for me to hear. "You aren't going to make it here," one would hiss. "We're going to ruin you and your family," another would murmur. "You're nothing but a fun-damn-mentalist," a bold tenor would say.

The stress began to take a physical toll. I'd perspire through my suits, which produced embarrassing armpit stains that were visible whenever I raised my arms. I would often have to change shirts and ties between services because I had drenched the first ones.

I went to a doctor for a checkup, and after looking at my results he asked, "Are you under a lot of stress or something?" I didn't know whether to laugh or cry. He told me I had a blood-pressure problem and needed medicine to control it. My thirty-two-year-old pride would have none of it. He insisted I have it checked each Sunday before I preached to make sure it didn't enter what he called "danger territory." So a registered nurse in our church, who was also sympathetic to my cause, checked me out each Sunday morning. At my insistence, she'd never tell me my blood pressure readings.

Still, the church was growing by bushels each week. I'd survived almost six months and thought I saw a light at the end of the tunnel. But then the train came roaring out of the darkness without warning. I was stuck. Motionless. The church was growing, and yet I was withering.

Trouble Looming

Memories are amazing things. Some imprint so vividly in our minds they remain HD-fresh even though they occurred in a

VHS world. One particular Sunday night in March is one of those memories.

When I was back in Mississippi preaching a revival, one of the members of the pastor search committee, a deacon, key leader, and friend, called me in a panic. "Pastor, I have some news, and I'm not sure if it's good or bad. The church administrator and worship leader resigned at the end of our services tonight saying they just couldn't work with you anymore."

My first reaction was relief. They were our two most influential staff persons and the ones leading the charge against me. But then the deacon said: "Be ready for some trouble." I didn't know it at that moment, but what he meant was be ready for some *trouble*. A steady rain of stress was about to turn into a tsunami that would threaten to sink my entire career. Maybe I should have stayed in Mississippi.

The next three weeks of my life were a roller coaster ride. But rather than highs and lows, I travelled between lows and lowers. You name it, I received it: hate mail, acrimonious meetings, threatening stares. The following Wednesday, I was told that a petition calling for my dismissal had reportedly attracted three hundred signatures. It was rumored that this petition was going to be presented at our quarterly business meeting scheduled for Sunday night.

Some of the key church leaders who supported me asked to meet that night to discuss the situation. I was hoping for a time of encouragement and inspiration, but instead they looked like a circle of death-row inmates just before the long walk to the gas chamber. My hopes for reassurance disappeared like a morning mist.

"Pastor," said one of the leaders, "we don't know what's going to happen Sunday night. There's a lot of unrest out there, but we're praying for you." What was left unsaid after the word *you* was, "in case you do get canned and your family is run out of town, even though you've done nothing wrong."

I walked out of that meeting dragging the weight of depression by the chain of uncertainty. My self-esteem was so low I would have needed a ladder just to get to the bottom.

My ten-minute drive home turned out to be more like Disney's "Mr. Toad's Wild Ride." Pulling into my garage, I noticed blue lights reflecting off my rearview mirror. Before I could get out to check the problem, I heard the police officer yell, "Don't get out of the car!"

I rolled down my window and my sunken eyes met the officer's.

"What's the matter with you!" he said. "Why didn't you pull over?"

"Pull over for what? What are you talking about?" I asked.

"You ran two red lights, one stop sign, and I clocked you speeding in two different speed zones!" he fired back, eyes ablaze.

I was incredulous, so focused on my problems that I didn't notice the world around me. Looking back, the grace of God protected me or I'd have killed myself or someone else.

"Officer, I am so sorry—"

"Driver's license and insurance card," he growled. Adding insult to embarrassment he added, "Have you been drinking?"

"Sir, I haven't had a drink in my life."

I'm not sure he believed me. He studied my driver's license for what seemed to be twenty minutes. He then asked, "Merritt...are you the pastor at First Baptist Church?"

"Uh, yes sir."

He ordered me to stay in my car until he returned. I watched him as he went back to his cruiser and began an earnest conversation with someone on his radio. He came back to my car, handed me my driver's license, and said, "Pastor Merritt, be more careful and have a nice evening."

I sat stunned.

"No ticket?"

Looking back with something between a sneer and a smile, he said, "My supervisor said you're in enough trouble as it is."

Showdown on Sunday

The sun peeked through our bedroom blinds the next morning, a Thursday, but I was already awake. Lying motionless. Staring at the ceiling. I rolled over to my wife and whispered in her ear, "Baby, I'm going to my study in the basement, and I don't want to be disturbed by anyone for anything. I don't care if President Reagan calls. No interruptions." When life knocks us down, we often feel alone and want to be alone.

I sat at my desk and stared at the cup of pens for a moment until my vision blurred. The tears began to dribble down my cheeks as I pushed back from my desk and slid off the chair until my knees hit the floor. Palms turned up and head hanging low, I prayed, "O God, if You have ever spoken to me before and if You never speak to me again, I need for You to speak to me today!"

> When life knocks us down, we often feel alone and want to be alone.

I grabbed two packs of 5x8 index cards, opened my Bible, and turned to the very first psalm. Having read these Hebrew hymns numerous times, I knew many of them were written by people well acquainted with hurt, heartache, and helplessness. I'd decided to spend the day reading all 150 psalms. I spent the entire day poring over each verse in each psalm as if I were searching for lost jewelry on a busy beach. Whenever I sensed that God was speaking to me, I would scribble that verse onto an index card.

At the end of the day, I went through every card, picked out my favorites, put the rest in a drawer, and walked back upstairs to await the showdown. Those next two days inched by at a caterpillar's pace, and I never went anywhere without my trusty cards. Every time fear would begin to creep into my heart, I would pull out a card, read it aloud, look up to Heaven and say, "Remember, God, You promised!" as if God might be suffering from amnesia.

Sunday afternoon finally arrived, and I paced nervously in my home office. I flipped through my cards like a gambler looking for a royal flush, stopping only occasionally to peer out the windows and check for circling vultures. Even though it was a cool spring afternoon, I was sweating as though I were in the middle of a desert town, dressed in a wool overcoat, and waiting for a gunfight with the local bandits. And perhaps I was.

The time finally arrived. I showered, changed into a fresh shirt and tie, draped my coat over my shoulder, kissed Teresa and my boys good-bye, and climbed into my car, as I had to go in early.

"We'll be all right," my wife said with a reassuring gaze. "You'll do great."

I made the longest ten-minute drive of my life—this time making sure I stopped at the stop signs and red lights. *No one comes to business meetings,* I told myself. *We've had two already and they were brief, uneventful, and sparsely attended. Maybe everyone will forget the meeting is tonight and I'll have worried over nothing.*

I started feeling good until I turned onto Church Street and saw a line of cars waiting to get into the crowded parking lot half an hour before the service started. The only elements missing were popcorn vendors and scalpers hawking tickets. To paraphrase Saddam Hussein, this was going to be the mother of all business meetings.

I walked directly to the baptistery to prepare to get into some lukewarm water to baptize several people, knowing that afterwards

I'd be standing in much hotter water. The service began at 5:59. I descended into the calm water and gazed out on the auditorium for the first time. The sight sent a shiver down to my feet.

In an auditorium that seated around seven hundred people, well over a thousand had gathered. I suspected they were not there to hear the great message I had prepared. They knew what I knew—no matter what else was happening tonight, this was going to be the best show in town. I knew how the Earps felt at the OK Corral.

After the baptism, I changed back into my suit and once again pored over my precious verses. I made my way down the stairs knowing what it must feel like to go to your own funeral. Sweat began to drip down my sides, as if my glands were hooked to an IV. I could feel my heart beating through my shirt. I put my hand on the door handle and prepared to enter a battlefield disguised as a worship center.

As I prepared to open that door, questions raced through my mind. *Why didn't I go to law school? That was all I dreamed about until God messed everything up. Why doesn't Jesus go ahead and return right now—two thousand years is long enough to keep a promise, right? Why didn't I become a Methodist or a Presbyterian? I should've known better.*

I reached for the door leading into the Lion's Den, and my knees almost buckled. I was convinced I would walk in fired up and walk out fired. But as I grabbed the handle, time began to slow and the God of tough times showed up and spoke up.

A verse that had not even made the cut on the cards I carried in my coat pocket leaped into my mind, a short verse from Psalm 56 that you'd likely miss if you weren't searching for it. David had written it after being captured by his enemies, the Philistines. I could almost hear the ancient king sing the words: "This I know, that God is for me."[1]

The next moment will always be one of the greatest of my life. Peace flooded my spirit, and I felt my heart rate slow. It was as if God and I were having our own private, intimate conversation. And then I said in my heart: *Lord, if they keep me, fine. If they fire me, fine. But I am not their hireling; I am Your man. Either way, I'm trusting You for my family and my future.*

The words were resounding: "This I know, that God is for me."

Trepidation gave way to trust, worry was replaced by worship, fear was conquered by faith. I knew that trouble rests in the hands of a sovereign God who will always stand beside me, within me, and most importantly for me.

I strode into the jam-packed auditorium and preached the sermon I'd prepared. I preached with the most joy and peace I'd had in the last six months. Seven people responded that night and surrendered to Christ, and when I finished, the show everyone came to see began.

Meeting Adjourned, Lesson Learned

I called the business meeting to order—yes, as the duly appointed moderator per the church policy manual, I was to preside at my own execution—and the crowd held their breath. After a couple of short perfunctory reports, I asked, "Is there any other old business?" The response was almost an audible "Are you kidding—we're here for the new business!" I paused, and then raised the question all had come to hear: "Is there any new business?"

A man who I knew opposed me slowly rose to his feet. I acknowledged him, and he surprisingly asked an innocuous question about the severance package for the worship leader who had resigned. One of the members of the personnel team that handled such matters answered with specifics on the generous severance package he'd been given. This seemed to satisfy if not mollify one of my most vocal critics.

He sat down, and I again asked: "Is there any other new business?"

The sweetest silence filled the auditorium. No one said a word. The spectators' faces began to show a mixture of relief, disappointment, and shock. Talk about anticlimactic! Trying to lighten the moment, I joked, "Going once, going twice…" Then one of the key leaders in the church, and one of my best friends, seized the moment and in a "let's not tempt fate here" voice shouted, "I move we adjourn!"

Of course that was the bell signaling the fight was over. Not only did no one land a punch on me, no one even threw one! Someone replied, "I second that motion." I was about to escape the lions with not even a scratch.

But in that moment, I realized why this tough time had come in my life. I knew I had to say one last thing to this church that I would end up serving for almost eighteen years.

"I need to say something before we leave," I said as people gathered their belongings.

Even my strongest supporters looked aghast.

"I want to say two things. First, I want you to know I am going to continue to preach the same way I have been preaching. Without fear or favor, I'm going to preach God's Word."

A terminally ill friend in the back stood up and yelled, "If you don't, I will vote to fire you!"

The next moment still gives me goose bumps. Except for maybe twenty or thirty people, the crowd rose to its feet and gave me a five-minute standing ovation. I have never fought back tears harder in my life than I did at that moment. It wasn't so much the applause that thrilled me but what it represented. I had faced the toughest time in my life, and God proved faithful as He saw me through.

The crowd sat back down, and I continued: "The second thing I want to say is that I am going to continue to lead this church the way I have been leading it."

The crowd gave me another ovation. And in that moment, I knew something had changed, and I had finally become the pastor of this church. The dust had settled, and by God's grace, I was still standing.

> Life's greatest lessons are learned in the midst of life's greatest struggles.

That wasn't the last tough time I would experience. The following Sunday I walked into a church where one-fourth of our total attendance (300 people) and almost half of our children's and students' Sunday school leadership didn't show up, never to return. I still received some mean-spirited letters and occasional dirty looks from former members when I would see them in the grocery store. But I learned a most memorable lesson, one not soon forgotten: life's greatest lessons are learned in the midst of life's greatest struggles.

In many ways the battlefield makes the soldier. How else can you discover your mettle as a warrior? Likewise, the storms of life test our character and resolve. Perhaps you're struggling with a crippling disease or crumbling marriage or embarrassing joblessness. Your situation may last far more than six months and may not end in applause, but you can be confident that the same One who bolstered me can sustain you too. The God who raised His Son from the dead on that glorious Sunday walks with us on those dreadful Mondays.

God never hints that we'll escape difficulties if we're smart enough, good enough, or lucky enough. Rather He promises and proves throughout the Bible that when tough times inevitably come, He will fight with us. And when the dust settles, regardless of the outcome, we can still stand.

"I have told you these things," Jesus said, "so that in me you may have peace. In this world you will have trouble. But take heart! I have overcome the world."[2]

You may be battling tough times in your office, school, home, or even church. I encourage you to take heart. Perhaps you languish in a hospital room, crippled by a debilitating disease. Jesus whispers to you: "Take heart."

You'll win some of life's skirmishes and lose others. But you don't have to fight alone. The One who has never lost a battle is fighting alongside you. When it's easier to sit down, sleep in, step aside, or slip away, God can help you stand tall. So let's discover together His winning strategies for facing tough times. Remember: Victory is never found in sitting out or running away. It's found in standing with the God who never fails.

2

When Life Is Physically Draining

"There is more to life than increasing its speed."

MOHANDAS GANDHI

I hear the ding on my phone indicating another email has come in, and my hand jumps to snatch it. The litany length of tomorrow's to-do list enlivens my mind such that I cannot sleep. When I consider the pile of bills on my kitchen table and the uncertainty of our volatile economy, I twitch in my seat.

I'm stressed, and if you're like most Americans, you are too. You're plagued by worry, racked with anxiety, and stalked by frustration. But admitting we share this problem doesn't solve much. We must decide what we will do about our stressful state of affairs.

Early in my career, I believed the solution for stress was management. Or perhaps suppression. Either way, it was an inevitable part of life that must be dealt with. But "dealing with it" is not a solution; that approach is a highway to breakdown.

In the recent movie *Limitless,* the main character, played by Bradley Cooper, happened upon a wonder drug that opened up the entire capacity of his brain. He could learn languages and complex math in a fraction of the time it took normal people. He could recall almost anything that he'd read or seen from the past.

He could analyze more quickly and more in-depth than the best financial gurus on the planet. He was limitless in his abilities. He was able to leverage this ability to earn millions and achieve great success.

As I watched this movie, I remember thinking, *Where can I get some of those pills? If only I could find a way to increase efficiency and accomplish more, all my problems would drift away.* I have a feeling that I'm not the only one who reacted to the film this way.

Fifty-four percent of Americans are concerned about the level of stress in their everyday lives. Sixty-two percent say work has a significant impact on their stress level. Seventy-three percent named "money" as the number one factor that affects their stress level.[1] I know I am dealing with a problem the majority of us face every day. But it's one thing to acknowledge that we all deal with stress and even suffer from it. It's another thing to tackle stress, controlling it instead of the reverse.

I've learned that you can categorize stress under three areas: *relational, financial,* and *occupational.* (I sympathize with you if you are saying, "I've hit the trifecta!") You are either *under pressure* or you are *under problems.* When you don't handle pressure well, you experience stress. When you don't handle problems well, you experience depression.

We now know that one of the major reactions to stress is depression. Some experts predict that depression will be the leading occupational disease of the twenty-first century. Some suggest depression will be responsible for more workdays lost than any other single factor. Today businesses in the U.S. spend $300 billion annually, or $7,500 dollars per employee, on stress related compensation claims, reduced productivity, absenteeism, health insurance costs, direct medical expenses, and employee turnover.[2]

I awaken early each morning—between five and six o'clock—focused on my to-do list and deadlines. I feel like a mosquito in a nudist colony: I don't know where to start! Tasks need finishing, concerns need addressing, problems need solving, emails need answering. And once I get done with all of these issues, I have to work on being a husband, father, grandfather, and friend.

I read about a guy who drove a small truck, transporting things for others in order to make a living. One day he was hired to transport some chickens. A guy in a car following the truck noticed something unusual about this truck driver. Every mile or so he would pull over, get out, and pound the side of the truck with a baseball bat. The guy in the car couldn't take it any longer. He stopped the guy and asked him why he was beating the side of the truck with a bat. "I've got a half-ton truck and a ton of chickens," the guy said. "I've got to keep half of them flying at all times!"

I feel like that a lot, as though I'm constantly beating my truck with a bat so half my chickens will stay in the air. I'm not asking you to throw a pity party and name me guest of honor. Instead, I want you to know that we struggle together. When you lie in bed late at night staring into the blackness, so do I. And when you wake an hour before your alarm is set to go off, I'm stirring with you. I deal constantly and consistently with stress. Sometimes it's caused by people and issues external to me. Other times it's self-induced and internal to me. I deal with it and I handle it, but I can never escape it completely.

My stress level concerns my wife. She's convinced it has taken years off my life. She constantly says, "I look forward to the day when you no longer face this problem." The "problem" is stress. The only comfort I find in the stress of my life is that I expect consternation as a pastor. It comes with the job.

Stress is almost a prerequisite to succeed in our culture. You want the corner office? Get ready for stress. A family? Stress will be your crest. Even planning a vacation to escape stress will wear you out. A life of strain seems inevitable.

But is it really?

Unfortunately, you're not Bradley Cooper's character and neither am I. We're not limitless. The sooner we get over this fact the better off we'll be. But I've discovered a strategy that's better than a fictional magic pill. I didn't find it in a self-help book or daytime television. It derives from one of the greatest leaders in all of history. This leader nearly burned out and died early because of his stress. Yet, he took three steps forward that gave him the ability to handle it all. And through this, he teaches us a winning strategy for overcoming a physically draining life.

Recognize Your Limits

Moses was literally in the middle of a *stress mess.* Here's the context.

> The next day Moses took his seat to serve as judge for the people, and they stood around him from morning till evening. When his father-in-law saw all that Moses was doing for the people, he said, "What is this you are doing for the people? Why do you alone sit as judge, while all these people stand around you from morning till evening?"
>
> Moses answered him, "Because the people come to me to seek God's will. Whenever they have a dispute, it is brought to me, and I decide between the parties and inform them of God's decrees and instructions."
>
> Moses' father-in-law replied, "What you are doing is not good. You and these people who come to you will only wear yourselves out. The work is too heavy for you; you cannot handle it alone."[3]

Moses was under a tremendous amount of stress, a word that comes from a Latin word meaning "to be drawn tight." I can't tell you how often I've felt entangled in a tightly drawn noose. But a word is more than its etymology. I define stress as *the gap between demands that are placed upon me in everyday life and the strength I have in meeting those demands.* Basically stress is the gap between my "ought tos" and my "can't dos."

The phenomenon is defined by others in various ways. Some call it the stress factor, and others the stress ratio. Many refer to it as the stress component or the stress formula. Whatever the best moniker is, we know that these pressures can drain us.

> Basically stress is the gap between my "ought tos" and my "can't dos."

Before we demonize Moses as someone who was a bad leader or poor at time management, let's admit that his stress was honestly earned. Sometimes we fall under stress we cause ourselves, stress that we really shouldn't be under. If you procrastinate and put something off until the last minute, you'll get stressed out. When you don't do what you ought to do, when you ought to do it, you will get stressed out. Laziness is a great stress producer—when you just don't do things at all and you let things go undone.

Moses was not lazy. He was getting into the office before sunup and he wasn't leaving until sundown. He was working six days a week, with no vacations, and no time off. He was the classic workaholic, but his fuel tank was empty. Not only had he reached his limits, he had exceeded them. Now he had to face his limits.

I don't care how much of a super-man or a super-woman you think you are, we all have limits. Indeed, the great philosopher Clint Eastwood, a.k.a. Dirty Harry, observed, "A wise man knows his limitations." Have you ever noticed on the back of a tractor-trailer rig the sign that communicates the load limit the truck can carry? That's one reason why highways have weigh stations along the way—to make sure these trucks aren't carrying more weight than they were designed to haul. If a tractor-trailer with a massive engine and unbelievable horsepower has load limits, then it makes sense that we do too.

This Jewish leader performed an impressive task. Eating on the run, ripping from one end of the camp to the other, planning appointments, meeting deadlines, and seeing everybody that wanted to see him. But on the inside he was dying. Each step of the way Moses moved closer to burnout. Maybe people close to Moses didn't notice it or didn't care, but Moses's father-in-law did both. He came to his son-in-law and said, "You and these people who come to you will only wear yourselves out."

The Hebrew word for "wearing out" literally means "to become old." Jethro was saying, "Moses, you're taking years off your life. You're growing old before your time. You're wearing yourself out unnecessarily."

One of the saddest things about the approaching death of the newspaper industry is the disappearance of comic strips. I remember finishing my *USA Today* when my kids were young and handing them the back page. There we'd sit with dirty dishes from Saturday breakfast before us, and I'd watch them chuckle.

A "Cathy" comic strip from years ago seems to illustrate how many people today feel. This homely single woman, who seems to be in her thirties or forties, is sitting at home with a typically disgruntled look on her face. She's pondering the many regrets she's facing from her workday, including things she wished she had said, and things she should have done for her family, friends, coworkers…and puppy.

At this point, you're feeling pretty sorry for the poor girl. And then comes the final frame with Cathy's conclusion:

Even when I'm not going any-where, I have three hundred pounds of luggage with me.

Do you ever feel like Cathy, as if you're carrying three hundred pounds of to-dos and didn't-dos on your back? I know I do. There are times when life gives me less than what I need and demands more than what I can give.

Years ago we bought a grandfather clock. We hired a professional, who works specifically with these types of clocks, to deliver that clock to our home. When he brought it to us and set it up, he told us we needed to avoid two dangers with this clock:

> Everyone must learn the art of separation. I must separate the pressures only I can handle from the ones that others can and should carry.

1. Don't let it run down.

2. Don't wind it too tight.

That's what happened to Moses and too often happens with each of us. We let ourselves run down and get wound too tight because we're carrying more of a load than God wants us to carry.

Whenever I begin to feel the weight of stress, I've made it a practice to take a step back and evaluate what's causing it. Once I pause, I discern whether I'm the one who ought to be handling those pressures at all. Everyone must learn the art of separation. That is, I must separate the pressures only I can handle from the ones that others can and should carry. If you try to handle everything, you won't handle anything very well.

Share the Load

When you're carrying too much of a load, you will eventually share that load one way or the other. Either you will collapse, unable to carry the load at all, *or* you will share a part of it so you can carry the load that you ought to be carrying. If the first step for dealing with a physically draining life is to recognize our individual limits, the second one is to learn to share the load. That was the advice Moses's father-in-law gave him:

> "Listen now to me and I will give you some advice, and may God be with you. You must be the people's representative before God and bring their disputes to him. Teach them his decrees and instructions, and show them the way they are to live and how they are to behave. But select capable men from all the people—men who fear God, trustworthy men who hate dishonest gain—and appoint them as officials over thousands, hundreds, fifties and tens. Have them serve as judges for the people at all times, but have them bring every difficult case to you; the simple cases they can decide themselves. That will make your load lighter, because they will share it with you. If you do this and God so commands, you will be able to stand the strain, and all these people will go home satisfied."[4]

Moses didn't realize it at the time, but Jethro just gave him one of the greatest leadership lessons ever taught or learned. He told Moses to evaluate what only he could do and delegate what others can do. Delegate to others what others can do so you can focus on the things that only you can do. Remember, nobody is indispensable, but everybody is important. Anytime you're looking at a job that looks bigger than you can handle alone, take that as a sign—God is telling you, don't try to do it alone.

This is common sense. If you're trying to lift a heavy load, both of your hands are better than one of your hands. Six hands are better than two. It's not the size of the job that causes stress. It's the sharing of a job that determines whether or not that job is stressful.

But something else arises from Jethro's instruction. He doesn't tell Moses to dump the work on just anybody. He emphasizes the importance of the people to whom Moses will delegate. More than just giving a job away, delegation entails ensuring the right person gets the right job. If you pair a person with a job that makes no sense to them, disaster will ensue.

When you delegate, you've got to do these things:

- Find the right people.
- Give them the right job.
- Trust them to do the right thing.
- Delegate the result, not the process.

I don't care how great you think you are or how indispensable you think you are to a company or an organization or a household or a PTA. Not even Moses, as great a man as he was, could do everything. One thing I'm constantly trying to master is to work smarter, not just harder. I work smarter by spending most of my time doing the things that I do best and doing the things that only I can do so that others can do what they do best and do what only they can do.

If you want to replace stress with serenity and pressures with peace, then *do only what you can do. Delegate the rest to others and leave the results to God.* That assertion does raise a question: "How do you separate those things you can do from what others can do? How do you determine how to prioritize what you need to be doing?"

Talk to God

Let's take a quick step back to the first piece of advice Jethro gave Moses: "Listen now to me and I will give you some advice, and may God be with you. You must be the people's representative before God and bring their disputes to him."[5]

Now we come to the root of Moses's problem. He was spending too much time talking to the people about God and not enough time talking to God about the people.

Who sets your schedule each day? One of three people will set your schedule. Either somebody else is going to set your schedule or you are going to set your schedule or you can go to God and ask Him to set your schedule. One of the reasons I believe that God allows us to get stressed out is to force us to come to Him for guidance and strength and direction.

There's plenty in life that I can't handle, but God and I together can handle anything. The key? Make sure to handle only the things God wants you to handle. If you're sitting there saying that you've got more to do at the end of every day than you can get done, then I can tell you one thing that is absolutely true about you. You are trying to do more than God wants you to do.

> There's plenty in life that I can't handle, but God and I together can handle anything.

We don't like to hear this kind of advice because we think we can handle the pressure. We fool ourselves if that's what we believe. And trust me, I don't like to hear this advice either. In my pride I think I can do it all. But I can't. It was a tough lesson for me to learn. But when I started to live by the lesson, I found my stress levels dropped and the kind of peace the Bible talks about—the peace that passes understanding—entered in. And that, my friend, is a beautiful place to be.

If you will indulge me, I want to put my pastor hat on for a moment. My mini-sermon for you right now is this: When you feel pressure from every side, like you're in stress's vise-grip, then listen up. Right there, in the middle of that stress, God is calling out to you saying, "If you will seek Me and spend time with Me and listen to Me, I will tell you what you need to do, and I will give you the power and the strength to do it."

When Moses did this, the Bible says, he would be able to stand the strain and all the people in his care would go home satisfied. The promise is not just extended to this great ancient leader, but to you as well.

Look at all the benefits Moses would receive if he handled stress God's way: longer life, working smarter, happier people, peace instead of pressure, sincerity instead of stress, work-life balance achieved. It only makes sense. God has things He wants you and me to accomplish day-by-day. If we focus on those things, He then is duty bound to give us the time, energy, and resources to do it.

Jesus is our greatest example here. He stayed in constant communication with His heavenly Father. He got his marching orders from Him daily. Yet in only three years of active ministry, He could look back and say, "I glorified you on earth, having accomplished the work that you gave me to do."[6]

Each day of your life you will accomplish nothing greater than to glorify God. Burning out, stressing out, falling out doesn't glorify God. Only doing the work He gives you to do daily glorifies Him.

In my opinion, the greatest coach ever, of any sport, is the late John Wooden. He won eleven national championships in thirteen years at UCLA. John Wooden introduced something in the early 1960s that was previously nonexistent in college basketball. He began to use the full-court press for almost the entire game. The relentless pressure against other teams caused many turnovers, and it helped bring Coach Wooden his first NCAA championship in 1964.

Coaches all over America began copying UCLA, but Coach Wooden said most coaches didn't really understand the purpose of the press. Other coaches assumed that the press was designed to create turnovers. Coach Wooden said that was never the design of the press. He said the press was installed to make the other team play at a faster tempo. Coach Wooden knew that, given the opportunity, most young players would play too fast, and that is when they make mistakes. More than any other lesson he taught, Coach Wooden constantly instructed his basketball teams to *slow down*. His motto was, "Be quick, but don't hurry."

Are you physically drained from the grind of life? Are you crumbling under the weight of stress? Do you feel drawn tight by the noose of your own schedule? You need to slow down and take a deep breath. You should evaluate your limits and do only what makes sense for you to do according to what you're best at. You should share the load and give away everything that somebody else can do. And you should remain in constant communication with the Lord.

At the end of *Limitless*, Bradley Cooper's character learned that even though his newfound ability produced immeasurable riches in his life, he could handle only so much. He also learned that to live limitless carried serious ramifications—side effects that damaged his very being. He eventually learned how to control the drug and to wean himself off it.

I made a decision about five years ago that I wish I had made at least twenty-five years before. I learned to say no. See, there was a time I thought every invitation to speak, counsel, consult, write, and advise had to be answered with a yes. I thought it would be neat to fly so often that the airline pilots would all know me by my first name. Then my wife and my executive assistant both came to the same conclusion—you can't go everywhere and be where you most need to be or accept everything and do what you most need to do.

I knew they were right. I cut my speaking almost in half and saw people only I could help or I really needed to see, and I was able to see more light than tunnel and more silver lining than cloud. Jesus accomplished the greatest work in history, finished *everything* His Father had assigned Him to do and did it completely stress free (except for the stress of the cross). What He did, He can enable us to do as well.

We weren't built to live without limits. We were built to live within the boundaries that God has established for us and to thrive in the work He's given us. And the truth of the matter is that when we do operate within ourselves and cling to God's strength, then and only then do we see the full extent and reach of our abilities.

Limitless? Doubtful. Stressless? Yes!

. . . .

Winning Strategy 1:
Find Others to Stand with You.

. . . .

3

When Life Is Dragging You Down

"One ceases to recognize the significance of mountain peaks if they are not viewed occasionally from the deepest valleys."

AL LORIN

When my family lived in Mississippi, I experienced what Saint John of the Cross referred to as the dark night of the soul. For months, life had been blissful. My oldest sons were five and two years old. Their cute faces and adoration greeted me each time I returned home from work. My precious wife, Teresa, showered me with abundant love. The church I pastored was growing,[1] my tennis game was improving, and I was in tip-top shape. Laurel, Mississippi, was in full bloom. The azaleas exploded with color, and lawns seemed to be painted green. Life wasn't perfect—I just told you I had two young children and was pastoring a church— but I had been, as they say, living the dream.

Then it happened.

I often refer to the day I crashed as "Black Monday" because the stock market of my life crashed. The previous night, I'd breathed in serenity. No out of the ordinary worries, no financial pressure, no health issues, and I couldn't remember the last time I needed to take a guilt trip. But I woke that morning coughing up despair.

No explanation exists for what happened that day. All I know is when my eyes opened to the morning sunbeams, I didn't want to get out of bed. I felt as if I'd been emotionally hijacked. My psyche weighed heavy, and my chest felt tight. Since I've always been an early riser, Teresa was shocked to roll over at 8:30 and see me lying in bed.

"Are you sick?" she asked.

I didn't know how to answer. I asked her if I felt feverish, hoping to be. Nope—I was as cool as the underside of a pillow.

"Is everything okay?" she said.

I was again at a complete loss for words. My mind wasn't well, that much I knew, but I couldn't explain what I felt. All I could tell her was that whatever it was, this was not going to be a "take an aspirin and call me in the morning" malady. And I was right. For three months, I would struggle with deep depression from which I could find no relief. Thus began the most difficult tough time I've ever faced.

We all have those "down in the dumps" days when nothing seems to go the way we'd wish. But then we meet a day when life spirals downward despite our best efforts to pull up. The thoughts in our mind swirl out of our control, and even the best self-talk seems useless. We walk slowly, dragging the weight of low self-esteem. We nurture shameful thoughts worsened by the reality that we can't share such things with anyone. Our hearts ache with loneliness or inexplicable anger. Though by all accounts we should be happy, we're deeply dissatisfied with our lives and ourselves.

I've never shared my struggle with depression before. The ordeal was too painful and embarrassing. I'm a pastor, after all, and believed in my younger years that I should appear untouched by such things. I still live with a nagging fear in the recesses of my mind that it could all happen again.

Sludging Through

I'd accepted that I was depressed, but I was determined not to let anyone know. Day after day, week after week, and month after month, I gave academy award winning performances. I faked everything: smiles, laughter, peace. Each morning I'd slide out of bed and slip a mask over my face that made me appear to have everything together. Each "Great!" or "Good to see you" was injected with extra oomph. But each day when I came home, I'd return the mask to its drawer and writhe again in frustrated pain. I felt as if I were walking in sludge up to my knees, carrying an over-filled backpack, enveloped in utter darkness.

Cry for help? Why would I? No one would care anyway.

Having struggled with depression actually places me into a large demographic. Roughly twenty million Americans are afflicted with depressive disorders,[2] and some experts claim that everyone will be affected by depression at some point in their lives.[3] A large proportion of the population wakes up each day in a cloud of gloom. They've visited the land of depression, and they know it's no vacation.

But too few people ever reach out for assistance. More than half of Americans believe depression is a personal weakness,[4] and 80 percent of depressed people aren't seeking any help.[5] The refusal to combat depression pushes those who suffer into a cycle of doldrums, a cycle of sadness and apprehension, a cycle that continues to carry them away into that limbo of hopelessness. Nothing is more depressing than being depressed.

The affliction is taking a toll on our nation. Businesses lose an estimated fifty billion dollars or more a year due to depressed workers, which either causes people not to work well or to miss work altogether. The average thirty-year-old American is ten times more likely to be depressed than their fathers and twenty times more like to be depressed than their grandfathers.[6]

> Nothing is more depressing than being depressed.

When my sons were younger, I used to read them a book called *Alexander and the Terrible, Horrible, No Good, Very Bad Day*. This slim volume recounted a boy's bout with a day where nothing seems to work out. Alexander falls asleep with gum in his mouth and finds it in his hair upon waking. His breakfast cereal lacked a toy in the bottom, and he can't seem to impress his schoolteacher despite his best efforts. He resolves several times to move to Australia.

Have you ever awakened in the morning with the knowledge that you were facing a terrible, horrible, no good, very bad day? Many people live day to day with that feeling in their stomach; they feel isolated and alone, beaten down and helpless, and worst of all hopeless.

Perhaps you've faced one of these scenarios:

- Your four-year-old comes into the kitchen and tells you she has just discovered oranges won't flush down toilets.

- Your birthday cake collapses from the weight of the candles.

- You go out to your garage to crank your car and the motor flies through your kitchen.

- You're following a group of Hell's Angels down the interstate when suddenly your car's horn goes off and remains stuck.

- You call your wife to tell her you want to eat out tonight, and when you get home you find a sandwich on the front porch.

- You wake up to discover that your waterbed has broken—then you remember you don't have a waterbed.

Obviously these are meant to be funny, but true depression is no laughing matter. If you're depressed, you need some wisdom on how to recover. Your situation won't be solved with a few clichés or a good pick-me-up lecture from a friend. You need wisdom delivered with a high degree of sensitivity and understanding. I'm not claiming to know all the answers, but I suggest we look to God's Word for encouragement and insight on how to wrestle through our dark nights of the soul.

I love the *realness* of the Bible. The ancient book doesn't see the world through rose-colored glasses, but rather paints an accurate picture of what authentic life actually looks like. It gives you not only the positive side of people; it shows you the negative side too. Whenever we talk about our family to others, we usually show the positive, only the best. The Bible, however, shows warts and all.

If the stories in the Bible contained people who were always good, great, and godly, who could relate? Even though this book talks so much about the people of God, it tells us that godly people have faults and problems and difficulties just like everybody else. In that sense, the Bible's honesty encourages me. If life is dragging you down, I'd like to introduce you to a prophet who helps teach us how to stand tall when we'd rather sleep through.

When Life Makes a Mess of Your Success

When we encounter Elijah in 1 Kings 19, he's in the middle of a furious pendulum swing. Having just been on top of the world, he nose-dives to the depths of depression. The prophet wrestles with how to cope and finds himself even nurturing thoughts of suicide.

Prior to this story, everything had been playing in Elijah's favor. He'd experienced one of the greatest single-handed victories in military or sports history. Four hundred and fifty false prophets of the pagan god Baal had challenged him to a duel, which Elijah accepted. A lone prophet of the one true God stands toe-to-toe with these false prophets in a spiritual contest and shows them all up. They call on their god to send fire down from Heaven, and all they hear is crickets. But when Elijah makes the same request of the God of Israel, a massive fireball falls from the sky and wows all who looked on. Afterward, Elijah slays them all, making him the MVP (Most Valuable Prophet) in the eyes of the nation.

Just before that, Elijah had predicted a nationwide drought. Because of the prophet's prayers, God turned off the atmospheric faucet and rain ceased to fall. When Elijah prayed again, God sent rain as if on cue. And on top of all this, he found time to raise the son of a widow from the dead. So from drought to death to disobedience, all he had known was uninterrupted success. As they say in sports, "He had the hot hand." Yet, like so many who find great success, he slipped into a depression.

Why the shift in disposition? He ran aground of an angry queen. A wicked king named Ahab ruled Israel with his wife, Jezebel. He was an evil king, but Jezebel turned out to be one of the most infamous women in history. She was not happy about Elijah killing her prophets, and she wasn't happy that God, through Elijah, was trying to turn the nation back to Him.

> Now Ahab told Jezebel everything Elijah had done and how he had killed all the prophets with the sword. So Jezebel sent a messenger to Elijah to say, "May the gods deal with me, be it ever so severely, if by this time tomorrow I do not make your life like that of one of them."[7]

Elijah had a contract on his life, but his response to Jezebel is key. He retreats inward—he goes into his shell—which is the knee-jerk response to both fear and depression. In life, mental distress often leads to physical retreat.

> Elijah was afraid and ran for his life. When he came to Beersheba in Judah, he left his servant there, while he himself went a day's journey into the wilderness. He came to a broom bush, sat down under it and prayed that he might die. "I have had enough, LORD," he said. "Take my life; I am no better than my ancestors." Then he lay down under the bush and fell asleep.
>
> All at once an angel touched him and said, "Get up and eat."[8]

Classic symptoms of being in the pits: crawl back into bed, pull the covers over your head, and throw a pity party. When you fall into depression, withdrawing seems like a logical solution. You can almost sense the evil one licking his chops when you go into your cave. After all, you don't want to fake it. You don't want to pretend that everything is fine—at least any more than you have to. So you isolate yourself. Been there, done that, and bought the factory that makes the T-shirts. But depression doesn't end when you disappear.

When Elijah withdraws, he learns that isolation doesn't dissipate depression; it deepens it. We find that truth in Elijah's life. Fortunately, God just didn't sit by and let the prophet wallow in his sty of self-pity. He poked and

> Classic symptoms of being in the pits: crawl back into bed, pull the covers over your head, and throw a pity party. But depression doesn't end when you disappear.

prodded a bit, and even spoke to him in a striking way. God told him exactly what he needed to hear.

You and I most likely will never experience a physical manifestation of God. If you encounter a burning bush like Moses did,[9] you should probably call the fire department. And if a donkey talks to you like one did to Balaam,[10] I'd suggest scheduling an appointment with your doctor. But the same God that spoke words of comfort to Elijah physically still speaks to us today scripturally, personally, and relationally. God still pursues us in our depressed state, often through our friends, family, and faith community.

Honesty Is the Best Policy

The first step of the famous Alcoholics Anonymous twelve-step program is *admission*: "We admitted we were powerless over alcohol—that our lives had become unmanageable." What is true for one's struggle with alcoholism is also true with depression. You must begin by acknowledging that a problem exists. For some reason, people like me don't like to admit they're depressed. Because of pride, embarrassment, shame, or a combination of those things, our reticence gets the best of us and we hide it.

Once you accept that you are depressed, you need to understand that you are not abnormal. Millions of Americans struggle with you. Psychologists tell us that after the year 2020, depression will be the second greatest killer of Americans after heart disease. Thirty percent of women are depressed. In fact, one psychologist has called it "the common cold of psychological disorders."[11]

You must also recognize that you are not ungodly. Some think depression is a sin and that Christians ought to be happy all the time. What a terrible and strange perspective to hold. Some of the greatest, godliest people in the Bible and in church history battled depression. Moses wrestled with it while leading the people of Israel. Job fell into it because of all the suffering he experienced. One of the greatest preachers who ever lived, Charles Haddon Spurgeon, called depression "the black dog" that followed him all his life. So take heart.

Like I said, depression touches each of us at some point in life. But if you are dealing with depression now, it will help you to pinpoint to what extent you suffer from it. There are different stages of depression:

- *Dejection*: A temporary emotional valley. Dejection doesn't last very long.

- *Discouragement*: A temporary feeling of hopelessness and a loss of enthusiasm that soon passes.

- *Despondency*: This produces intense melancholy feelings that can last for weeks or even months. Sometimes it can cause you to quit eating or insomnia.

- *Despair*: A perilous stage of emotional instability where pessimistic feelings and even suicidal thoughts can overwhelm you. This is the most serious and dangerous stage of depression.[12]

If you are in any of these stages, or if your depression has deepened to one of the later stages, I want to encourage you to take steps to climb out of it. Find the strength to admit it to yourself and then admit it to God, since He already knows. Then, if you can find someone you love or trust, admit it to him or her. Get their advice whether you should seek the help of a professional. You owe it to yourself, your family, and your friends to be the best you can be. No amount of pride is worth walking every day under the black cloud of depression.

As Catholic theologian Henri Nouwen has written:

> So often we are inclined to keep our lives hidden. Shame and guilt prevent us from letting others know what we are living. We think: "If my family and friends knew the dark cravings of my heart and my strange mental wanderings, they would push me away and exclude me from their company."
>
> But the opposite is true. When we dare to lift our cup and let our friends know what is in it, they will be encouraged to lift their cups to share with us their anxiously hidden secrets. The greatest healing often takes place when we no longer feel isolated by our shame and guilt and discover that others often feel what we feel and think what we think and have the fears, apprehensions, and preoccupations we have.[13]

Don't let isolation or pride keep you from conquering your depression. When you can muster the strength to be honest with yourself and others, you'll find healing on the other side.

Pose the Question, Why?

When I was depressed, I forced myself to take the time necessary to discover the why behind my condition. I analyzed possible causes and took a careful look at how I was dealing with it. This turned out to be one of the most uncomfortable and liberating exercises of my life. Most of us never take the time for serious self-evaluation; when we do, we'll learn much about ourselves. At the same time, looking at your life can be frustrating. You begin to notice all the warts that you pass over most days, and you realize afresh your own humanity and brokenness.

Some of the whys of depression look different than expected. It's not unusual, for example, to fall into depression right after a great success or right after a great victory, just as Elijah did. You can't be up all the time. That's why you will watch your favorite football team beat their toughest rival one week and then barely overcome an inferior opponent the next. Some of my toughest times came after my best days. In fact, I have to battle depression somewhat when I come off vacation and have just had the time of my life.

Sometimes a crisis moment can cause depression. Perhaps a close friend betrays you and you grow angry. Psychologists say repressed anger, or what we call bitterness, is the number one cause of depression. People get bitter and angry with others, at themselves, or even at God. They internalize it. Their bitterness deepens and they get depressed. In response, your emotions can crash, leaving you in a state of depression.

In my ministry experience, I meet many who suffer from what I call "3-D depression"—that is, depression caused by divorce, death, or disaster. A loved one passes unexpectedly or at an early age, the tumor is malignant, or a spouse informs you they don't love you anymore.

In my research, both biblical and extrabiblical, I've discovered three basic causes of depression not related to crisis moments. First, there can be a *physical* cause to depression. Elijah dealt with this. He was worn out: weak, hungry, exhausted. Having just come off a long fast, his body was weakened. He had also just run eighteen miles to deliver the good news of his victory over the pagan prophets. He was physically weak.

One of the best life practices to combat depression is exercise. If you rise early each morning, eat on the run, work seven days a week, and never exercise, don't be surprised if your body reacts negatively. If you're a stay-at-home parent with small children, unending household duties, and crying babies, your body can react. So a physical component often lies behind depression.

Mental distress can also stem from a *chemical* cause. When the brain's chemical messengers, called neurotransmitters, are healthy, we are too. When some of those transmitters—such as serotonin or dopamine—are absent, low, or imbalanced, it can trigger major depression.

And you cannot discount *spiritual* causes of depression. Satan wants God's people depressed. Often spiritual warfare is either at the root of our problems or is exacerbating them.

Do any of these causes sound familiar to you? Can you relate? I encourage you to take the next step and analyze your problem. Make sure you've done everything in your power to root out the problem. Find out whether it is a physical, emotional, or spiritual problem. Have you been able to pinpoint the cause(s) either potentially or actually? Then it's time to take the last step to get out of the pit and back on the road to peace of mind and productivity of life.

The Best Defense Is a Good Offense

Being depressed isn't wrong, but staying depressed can be. Jesus Christ said He came that we might have joy—a joy the Bible calls "inexpressible and glorious."[14] Elijah overcame his depression. God restored joy to his life. Elijah took three practical steps that you can take as well.

First of all, *refresh yourself.*

> Then [Elijah] lay down under the bush and fell asleep. All at once an angel touched him and said, "Get up and eat." He looked around, and there by his head was some bread baked over hot coals, and a jar of water. He ate and drank and then lay down again.[15]

Elijah took a nap and then ate a good meal. If you can learn to rest and relax, you'll find that R & R will do wonders for you both spiritually and physically. I decided a few years ago to take a month off every summer. This practice has figuratively saved my life, giving me the strength to give my best during the other eleven months. Martin Luther said one time, "I have so much to do today I simply must go back to bed." Sometimes, rest can work wonders—both physically and mentally.

God also fed the famished prophet who had not eaten for days. Sometimes the greatest remedy for depression is just some old-fashioned refreshment. Your mother was right: getting adequate rest along with eating a balanced diet can work wonders for your life.

> Your mother was right: getting adequate rest along with eating a balanced diet can work wonders for your life.

The second thing is *focus on God*. Elijah made a mistake when he began to focus on himself. " 'I have had enough, Lord,' he said. 'Take my life; I am no better than my ancestors.' "[16]

Elijah completely lost sight of God. He was attending the one type of party you should never attend: a pity party. Don't forget this. God doesn't throw pity parties. When you take your eyes off God and focus instead on yourself, you will start experiencing what Zig Ziglar calls "stinkin' thinkin'." You will exaggerate every problem you face and totally forget the One who can solve any problem you have. That's exactly what Elijah had done.

> [On Mount Horeb] he went into a cave and spent the night.
> And the word of the Lord came to him: "What are you doing here, Elijah?"
> He replied, "I have been very zealous for the Lord God Almighty. The Israelites have rejected your covenant, torn down your altars, and put your prophets to death with the sword. I am the only one left, and now they are trying to kill me too."[17]

Elijah was singing a familiar tune: "I am all alone and nobody cares. La-da-dee, la-dee-da." Ever sing that song? I have. But then God changes his tune.

> The Lord said, "Go out and stand on the mountain in the presence of the Lord, for the Lord is about to pass by."
> Then a great and powerful wind tore the mountains apart and shattered the rocks before the Lord, but the Lord was not in the wind. After the wind there was an earthquake, but the Lord was not in the earthquake. After the earthquake came a fire, but the Lord was not in the fire. And after the fire came a gentle whisper.[18]

God helped Elijah quit thinking about himself and his problems and start thinking about God. When God has your ear, He can speak into it. When God has your heart, He can minister to it. Depressed people always look down, but we must learn to look up. That's why Scripture reading is so important when you're struggling with depression. If life is dragging you down, and you're ready to stand back up, climb into God's Word, claim His promises, ask His help, and talk plainly with Him. But prepare for wondrous things to occur. Instead of focusing on all the burdens you bear, a new focus will arise. An air of thankfulness will wash over you as you bring God and His glory back into the picture.

Finally, *attend to others.*

> The Lord said to him, "Go back the way you came, and go to the Desert of Damascus. When you get there, anoint Hazael king over Aram. Also, anoint Jehu son of Nimshi king over Israel, and anoint Elisha son of Shaphat from Abel Meholah to succeed you as prophet."[19]

God not only gave Elijah something to do besides just sitting around and feeling sorry for himself, but He also gave him someone to minister to. He gave him someone to serve. Some kings needed the anointing of God in their life and only Elijah could perform the task. When life has us down in the dumps, sometimes we need only find a diversion, a job to fill our time and allow us to stop thinking about what ails us.

Perhaps you need to find someone to minister to. Remember that you're not the only one in this world who has problems. There are people out there worse off than you are. They need someone like you to come alongside them and, if nothing else, let them know you can relate to how they feel. They need someone like you to minister to them, to encourage them. If you want to see the fog of depression lifted, quit looking in the mirror and start looking out the window.

Someone once went to Karl Menninger, the leading psychiatrist of the latter part of the twentieth century, and asked, "What would you advise a person to do who is experiencing deep depression and unhappiness?" The questioner expected Dr. Menninger to answer with something like, "Go see a psychiatrist." To this person's amazement, Menninger said, "Lock the door behind you. Go across the street. Find somebody that has a need and do something to help them."

If you are depressed, discouraged, dejected, or defeated, go to your doctor and make sure you're physically healthy and chemically balanced. Then go into the street and find someone worse off than you. Help others when you need help yourself. And be sure to go to God. Reflect on His blessings. Instead of griping about what you don't have, be thankful for what you do have.

Do that and watch the beautiful salve of thankfulness and service pour over you, releasing you from your struggle and giving rise to a person reborn—full of life and gleaming with God's love.

• •

Winning Strategy 2:
Stand Aside and Take a Break.

• •

4

When Life Is Unfair

"Adversity is a fact of life. It can't be controlled.
What we can control is how we react to it."

Anonymous

You exercise close to the recommended twenty minutes a day, live in the state where you were born, and spend more money in restaurants than grocery stores. Your showers last approximately ten minutes, and you spend 95 percent of your day indoors. You surf the Internet for two and a half hours every day, encountering celebrities that you will outlive by thirteen years because they are four times more likely to commit suicide.

You will consume twenty teaspoons of added sugar today, which is unfortunate since you won't floss. But perhaps God can supernaturally protect your enamel. You do believe in Him after all. And at some point during the day you will say a prayer.

Who is the "you" I'm talking about? It's you. It's me. It's the average Joe in America.[1] We're all so much alike and all so very different from one another. But if there's one thing I know we all need, it's how to face adversity in this life.

Some things about me you'd probably chuckle at, like my basement. I have an awesome basement that is wall-to-wall Georgia Bulldogs. From the light fixtures to the trophy case to the wall color, it's a one-of-a-kind basement and I love it. In that regard, I'm unique. I'm different from you. You and I both like what we like and those preferences make us one-of-a-kind. But you and I also deal with family pressures, life pressures, work pressures, and "I don't deserve this" pressures. In some ways those are the worst kind.

"What do you mean I have lung cancer? I've never smoked a day in my life."

"You're leaving me for someone else and you admit it's all your fault…so why am I the one getting the shaft?"

"You're laying me off only one year before my retirement is fully vested after thirty years of faithful service?"

These situations confront us average Joes every day. If we live long enough, we all get what we don't deserve.

In the Bible, we encounter an average Joe who shines light on how to deal with life when it's unfair. Joseph was a lot like us. He had a unique family situation, but he also dealt with some pressures that I'm sure you have already dealt with or will someday.

He was one of twelve sons of Jacob, who happened to be the grandson of Abraham, the founder of the Hebrew nation. Had you lived in Joseph's time, you would have seen just how average he was. There was nothing special about him. He wasn't royalty. He wasn't a celebrity. Although his father was financially well off, Joseph was no Donald Trump. Have you heard of Joe the Plumber? Well, meet Joe the Shepherd.

When you look at Joseph's life in the Bible, it screams out to be studied. Just look at how much of the Scriptures are given to the creation of the galaxies: "[God] also made the stars."[2] That's it. Five words! It's almost as though it were an afterthought. Weigh those five words against the fourteen chapters given to Joseph. God wants us to notice this Average Joe's life and learn something from it.

We first meet Joseph in Genesis 37:

> This is the account of Jacob's family line.

Joseph, a young man of seventeen, was tending the flocks with his brothers, the sons of Bilhah and the sons of Zilpah, his father's wives, and he brought their father a bad report about them.[3]

On the outside, even his family seemed average. He had eleven brothers. And when you look closely at his family, you find they were one of the first dysfunctional families in recorded history.

Getting What You Don't Deserve

Imagine you are Joseph. You share a father with your siblings, but four different mothers have given birth along the way. Not only do you come from a large family, but it's more blended than the Brady Bunch. Your dad's a con artist—has been his whole life and everyone knows it. The whole community knows he cheated your uncle out of the estate and then hid behind his mother's skirts, as we like to say in the south, before running off like a coward to avoid being killed. Your great uncle tricked your dad into marrying your mother's sister, perhaps by getting your dad so drunk during the wedding feast that he didn't know which sister he married. He wound up marrying the ugly one instead of the pretty one, but that didn't faze him. He just married both of them! The one he really loved couldn't have kids, so he slept with the nanny. He enjoyed it so much he started sleeping with most of the kitchen help too. No wonder you always thought your brothers looked like the cooks![4]

You're finally born to the bride that your dad wanted to marry in the first place. Immediately you rise to the top—your dad's favorite son. All your brothers recognize it, which creates a lot of family drama. You get the BMW and they get bicycles. You get the king-sized cot and they get sleeping bags. As a country singer once opined, you get the gold mine and they get the shaft. To top it off, you rub it in their faces by describing for them dreams you've had about how special you are. Eventually, they get sick of hearing about it and take action:

> So when Joseph came to his brothers, they stripped him of his robe—the ornate robe he was wearing—and they took him and threw him into the cistern. The cistern was empty; there was no water in it.
>
> As they sat down to eat their meal, they looked up and saw a caravan of Ishmaelites coming from Gilead. Their camels were loaded with spices, balm and myrrh, and they were on their way to take them down to Egypt.
>
> Judah said to his brothers, "What will we gain if we kill our brother and cover up his blood? Come, let's sell him to the Ishmaelites and not lay our hands on him; after all, he is our brother, our own flesh and blood." His brothers agreed.
>
> So when the Midianite merchants came by, his brothers pulled Joseph up out of the cistern and sold him for twenty shekels of silver to the Ishmaelites, who took him to Egypt.[5]

No, this is not a script from Hollywood. This is not an ancient protoscript for *Keeping Up with the Kardashians*. This is the life of our average Joe.

As we often do, Joseph got what he didn't deserve. Sure, he'd been difficult to live with, bragged too much, and flaunted the favoritism of his dad. But even that doesn't warrant being sold by his brothers to foreign traveling salesmen for the price of a bag of groceries, getting carted off to a foreign land surrounded by people he didn't know who speak a language he doesn't understand in a culture he has never seen. This isn't a simple story of sibling rivalry that ended in a roll in the mud. It's a cruel tale of hate and revenge.

Joseph's misfortune reminds us that every person experiences good days and bad days, up times and down times. But what really matters is how we respond to the bad times as well as the good.

When I read this story my mind jumps into question mode. How did Joseph feel when his brothers sold him? How did he deal with that rejection? What would I do? I see Joseph carted off to a foreign country and I wonder what I can learn from his response to his low Valley-of-Death time of life.

> You're going to get what you don't deserve. The question you must answer is, "How will I deal with it?"

You and I may not know what it's like to get sold into slavery, but we can relate to what it feels like when we get what we don't deserve. *That* happens to all of us. Somebody else gets the promotion. You get let go even though you have seniority at work. You get falsely accused. You're blamed for someone else's mistake. Just fill in the blank.

It's going to happen. You're going to get what you don't deserve. The question you must answer is, "How will I deal with it?"

God Stands Beside You

One of the hardest things about getting what we don't deserve is that alone feeling that seeds itself in our gut. Joseph could relate. Here's the scene:

> Now Joseph had been taken down to Egypt. Potiphar, an Egyptian who was one of Pharaoh's officials, the captain of the guard, bought him from the Ishmaelites who had taken him there.[6]

For Joseph every foreseeable day is a bad one. He's living in a foreign land, working for a master he's never met. He cooks his food, cleans his house, washes his clothes, runs his errands, and his life has become a meaningless meandering of the mundane. Can you imagine?

But then the story explodes with just one statement: "The LORD was with Joseph."[7]

Where did those words come from? In the midst of all that Joseph's experienced, the last thing we're expecting to read is that God was with him through it all. Here's Joseph, a good guy stuck to work as a slave, sleeping on the ground with the other hired help. Meanwhile the really bad guys—his brothers—are back home grilling hamburgers and playing golf, sleeping in their own homes, in their own beds. Something's not right with this picture.

And maybe it's the same thing wrong with your picture. You still wonder, *Why did she marry him instead of me? Why didn't I get the promotion? Why did my two best friends get into the college I wanted to attend, but I didn't? Why did his pension plan survive but mine didn't?*

And then those five words arrest us: "The LORD was with Joseph."

We begin to breathe easy. God is with Joseph. Things should start turning around for him, right? Wrong. They get worse. And this is difficult for us to understand because we assume that having God's presence should assure smooth sailing. What's hard about getting what we don't deserve is when we believe that God is with us, and yet things persist or even get worse as was the case for Joseph.

> Now Joseph was well-built and handsome, and after a while his master's wife took notice of Joseph and said, "Come to bed with me!"
>
> But he refused. "With me in charge," he told her, "my master does not concern himself with

anything in the house; everything he owns he has entrusted to my care. No one is greater in this house than I am. My master has withheld nothing from me except you, because you are his wife. How then could I do such a wicked thing and sin against God?" And though she spoke to Joseph day after day, he refused to go to bed with her or even be with her.[8]

Temptation confronts Joseph head-on—a temptation stronger than Hercules on steroids. Joseph is Brad Pitt and Potiphar's wife is Angelina Jolie. Once again, Joseph is in a no-win situation. And he realizes it. If he sleeps with her and Potiphar finds out, he'll be executed on the spot. If he resists, he will land himself on Mrs. Potiphar's bad side, and one can only guess where that will lead.

Keep in mind that Joseph knows that God is walking beside him. Joseph knows that God is over these circumstances. God is behind the scene. So Joseph responds to the circumstance accordingly. He does what you and I will do when we're convinced of God's presence in our lives. You do right regardless of the cost. Joseph chooses trust over lust. He chooses obedience over expedience. And his bold stand reminds us that our conduct always reveals the level of confidence we have in God's abiding presence.

From the outside, it didn't appear God was with Joseph. If He was, He wasn't doing a good job—or so it seemed. But Joseph knew what we must know: God *is* with you even when there is no evidence that He is. Even when

> God's way isn't to make everything okay. God's way is to give us the strength to endure and the vision to see that our circumstances—no matter how dire or grim—are never as big as He is.

you are getting what you don't deserve, God is walking beside you. That's been my experience. I know it might be hard to believe at times. But trust me, it's the truth. God's way isn't to make everything okay. God's way is to give us the strength to endure and the vision to see that our circumstances—no matter how dire or grim—are never as big as He is.

God Works for You

Potiphar's wife continues to pursue Joseph, trying everything she can to get him into bed. But he refuses. One day, in a final act of desperation, she literally grabs him by his coat in an attempt to drag him to her bed. He runs out of the house so fast that he leaves his coat behind. Remember the old saying, "Hell has no fury like a woman scorned"? Well, Joseph is about to experience the truth of this axiom firsthand!

As soon as Potiphar returns home, his wife lies and says that Joseph tried to rape her. Take a guess: How do you think this is going to turn out for our average Joe?

> When his master heard the story his wife told him, saying, "This is how your slave treated me," he burned with anger. Joseph's master took him and put him in prison, the place where the king's prisoners were confined.[9]

Joseph's journey thus far goes from the pit to the prison. Incredibly, he does the right thing, makes the right decision, takes the right path—and still gets burned! Remember, this is not America. Ancient Egypt had no Fifth Amendment guarantee, no right to a fair trial, no Miranda rights, and no phone call. He is declared guilty with no chance of proving his innocence. Worse, Joseph has done nothing wrong other than a little strutting around in front of his brothers. But even in this dark moment, we hear the echoing encouragement again: "the Lord was with him."[10]

If I had been standing in Joseph's shoes, I would have told God: "If it's all the same to You, I'd rather not have You walking with me. Since You've been with me, I've gone from being thrown in a pit, to being sold into slavery, to being put in prison for a crime I didn't commit. This relationship doesn't seem to be working out." Knowing my temperament, I probably would have added, "In fact, God, why don't You go be with my brothers!"

But before we start ranting about the things happening to us that we don't deserve, before we start complaining to God, we must ask a key question: *Would I rather be on the beach in Hawaii, drinking pineapple juice, soaking in the sun, and outside of God's will, or falsely accused in a foreign prison inside of God's will?*

It's hard to see, in Joseph's scenario, how God is walking beside him. But it's even more difficult to admit that God is actually *working* for Joseph.

"How?" you ask. "What is God actively doing to help him? He's in prison, for crying out loud. If this is the best God can do, maybe He should get into a new line of work."

In order to understand the betrayal and the pit and the slavery and the prison time, you have to see things from God's point of view. This is a difficult task because human minds are so unlike God's. And this is a good thing. If God acted or reacted like I do, we'd all be in a heap of trouble. I've found that when I exercise some patience, I eventually gain His vision and see His plan.

Fast-forward ten years, and while Joseph is still incarcerated, an incredible turn of events takes place. Through contacts Joseph made in prison, contacts he would not have made outside of prison, he receives an unexpected appointment with Pharaoh regarding a dream that troubled him. God helps Joseph interpret Pharaoh's dream and predict the future for the entire country. What happened next could happen only if God were with you working for you:

> Then Pharaoh said to Joseph, "Since God has made all this known to you, there is no one so discerning and wise as you. You shall be in charge of my palace, and all my people are to submit to your orders. Only with respect to the throne will I be greater than you."
>
> So Pharaoh said to Joseph, "I hereby put you in charge of the whole land of Egypt." Then Pharaoh took his signet ring from his finger and put it on Joseph's finger. He dressed him in robes of fine linen and put a gold chain around his neck. He had him ride in a chariot as his second-in-command, and people shouted before him, "Make way!" Thus he put him in charge of the whole land of Egypt.[11]

In a meeting that took less than twenty minutes, Pharaoh makes Joseph prime minister of the entire country—second in authority only to him! Pharaoh's act catapulted Joseph from the pit to the palace. God works, in hindsight, through a beautiful story arc. His way of getting Joseph to the palace was through the pit and the prison. As with Joseph, what we so often see as stumbling blocks are really stepping-stones God uses to accomplish His plan and fulfill His purpose for our lives.

> What we so often see as stumbling blocks are really stepping-stones God uses to accomplish His plan and fulfill His purpose for our lives.

We need to accept an inevitable fact: *We are going to get what we don't deserve.* Somewhere, somehow, and at some time. But you can remain standing if you respond to these times as if God is *walking beside you* and believe that God is *working for you.* If you and I can respond like that, then something beautiful happens. The world sees God in us.

God Speaks Through You

The way we react to life's circumstances says a lot about us. Our actions, as is true so often, speak louder than our words. The same was true for Joseph. If we take a quick look back in his story, we read some revealing observations regarding Joseph's testimony.

> The LORD was with Joseph so that he prospered, and he lived in the house of his Egyptian master. When his master saw that the LORD was with him and that the LORD gave him success in everything he did, Joseph found favor in his eyes and became his attendant. Potiphar put him in charge of his household, and he entrusted to his care everything he owned.[12]

Joseph's boss, Potiphar, saw something in Joseph that others will see in you when you act and live as if God is *walking beside you* and *working for you* no matter what happens to you. Unlike the other foreign slaves that Potiphar bought, Joseph did not sulk or complain or gripe or moan about his circumstances. He trusted that God was with him. Joseph lived every day with a belief that you couldn't shake with a hurricane: God was in charge.

Even in prison, the warden put Joseph in charge of the other prisoners because the Lord was with him. Joseph didn't require supervision because he was a man of integrity. His character was evident and respected by the very men who were charged with watching him. Imagine a warden trusting a prisoner in this way. Unbelievable.

A pattern is developing. Joseph becomes everybody's favorite. Not just his dad's favorite, but Potiphar's favorite and the warden's favorite, and finally Pharaoh's favorite. What was so different about him than everybody else? Joseph was confident that God was walking beside him and working for him. And he lived accordingly.

When you and I believe and act as Joseph did, we'll experience God *speaking through us*. Others will see our trust and our faith and our peace in uncertainty and unfairness. They will see the God we *say* we believe through the way we *live*. Indeed, one of the reasons God allows tough times into our lives is to give us the chance to show others how to meet Him.

Joseph spent a total of thirteen years in prison, a fact often passed over in this story. Remember why he was there. It started with jealous brothers, a lying and lustful woman, and an ungrateful cupbearer. Just as our average Joe found out in this story, the arithmetic of life does not always add up. We will get what we don't deserve, but we must determine how to respond.

In 1921, a missionary couple named David and Svea Flood went with their two-year-old son David from Sweden to the heart of Africa—to what was then called the Belgian Congo. They met up with another young Scandinavian couple, the Ericksons, and the four of them sought God for direction. They felt led of the Lord to go out from the main mission station and take the gospel to the remote village of N'dolera. When they arrived, the chief rebuffed them and would not let them enter his village for fear of alienating the local gods. The two couples opted to go half a mile up the slope and build their own mud huts.

They prayed for a spiritual breakthrough, but there was none. Their only contact with the villagers was a young boy, who was allowed to sell them chickens and eggs twice a week. Svea Flood, a tiny woman only four feet, eight inches tall, decided that if this was the only African she could talk to, she would try to lead the boy to Jesus. And in fact, after many weeks of loving and witnessing to him, he trusted Christ as his Savior.

Meanwhile, malaria struck one member of the little band after another. In time the Ericksons decided they had had enough suffering and returned to the central mission station. David and

Svea remained near N'dolera to go on alone. Then, of all things, Svea found herself pregnant in the middle of the primitive wilderness. When the time came for her to give birth (1923), the village chief softened enough to allow a midwife to help her. A little girl was born, whom they named Aina.

The delivery, however, was exhausting, and Svea was already weak from bouts of malaria. The birth process was a heavy blow to her stamina. After seventeen desperate days of prayer and struggle, she died.

Something snapped inside David at that moment. His heart full of bitterness, he dug a crude grave, buried his twenty-seven-year-old wife, and took his children back down the mountain to the mission station. Giving his newborn daughter to the Ericksons, he said, "I'm going back to Sweden. I've lost my wife, and I can't take care of this baby. God has ruined my life." With two-year-old David, he headed for the coast, rejecting not only his calling but God Himself.

Within eight months, both the Ericksons were stricken with a mysterious illness (some believe they were poisoned by a local chief). They died within days of each other. Nine-month-old Aina was given to an American missionary couple named Berg, who adjusted her Swedish name to Aggie and eventually brought her back to the United States.

The Bergs loved little Aggie but were afraid that if they tried to return to Africa, some legal obstacle might separate her from them since they had been unable to legally adopt her. So they decided to stay in the U.S. and switch from missionary work to pastoral ministry. And that is how Aggie grew up in South Dakota. She attended North Central Bible College in Minneapolis where she met and married a young preacher named Dewey Hurst.

Years passed and the Hursts enjoyed a fruitful ministry. Aggie gave birth first to a daughter, then a son. In time her husband became president of a Christian college in the Seattle area. Aggie was intrigued to find so much Scandinavian heritage there.

One day around 1963, a Swedish religious magazine appeared in her mailbox. She had no idea who sent it, and she couldn't read the words. But as she turned the pages, all of a sudden a photo stopped her cold. There in a primitive setting in the heart of Africa was a grave with a white cross and on the cross was her mother's name, Svea Flood.

Aggie jumped in her car and drove straight to a college faculty member who, she knew, could translate the article. "What does this say?" she asked.

The instructor translated the story: "It tells about missionaries who went to N'dolera in the heart of the Belgian Congo in 1921...the birth of a white baby girl...the death of the young missionary mother...the one little African boy who had been led to Christ...and how, after all the whites had left, the little African boy grew up and persuaded the chief to let him build a school in the village."

The article said that gradually the now grown-up boy won all his students to Christ, the children led their parents to Christ, and even the chief had become a Christian. Today (1963) there were six hundred Christian believers in that one village.

Because of the willingness of David and Svea Flood to answer God's call to Africa, because they endured so much but were still faithful to witness and lead a single boy to trust Jesus, God had saved 600 people. And the boy, as a grown man, became head of the Pentecostal Church and leader of 110,000 Christians in Zaire.

At the time Svea died, it appeared to human reason that God had led the young couple to Africa only to desert them in their time of deepest need. It would be forty years before God's amazing grace and His real plan for the village of N'dolera would be known.

For Dewey and Aggie Hurst's twenty-fifth wedding anniversary, the college presented them with the gift of a vacation to Sweden. There Aggie met her biological father. An old man now, David Flood had remarried, fathered four more children, and generally dissipated his life with alcohol. He had recently suffered a stroke. Still bitter, he had one rule in his family: "Never mention the name of God because God took everything from me."

After an emotional reunion with her half-brothers and half-sister, Aggie brought up the subject of seeing her father. The others hesitated.

"You can talk to him," they said, "even though he's very ill now. But you need to know that whenever he hears the name of God, he flies into a rage."

Aggie could not be deterred. She walked into the squalid apartment, with liquor bottles everywhere, and approached the seventy-three-year-old man lying in a rumpled bed.

"Papa?" she said tentatively.

He turned and began to cry.

"Aina," he said, "I never meant to give you away."

"It's all right, Papa," she said, taking him gently in her arms. "God took care of me."

The man instantly stiffened. The tears stopped.

"God forgot all of us. Our lives have been like this because of Him."

He turned his face back to the wall. Aggie stroked his face and continued.

"Papa, I've got a little story to tell you, and it's a true one. You didn't go to Africa in vain. Mama didn't die in vain. The little boy you both won to the Lord grew up to win that whole village to Jesus Christ. The one seed you planted just kept growing and growing. Today there are six hundred African people serving the

Lord because you and Momma were faithful to the call of God on your life."

She paused.

"Papa, Jesus loves you. He has never hated you."

The old man turned back to look into his daughter's eyes. His body relaxed. He began to talk. And by the end of the afternoon, he had come back to the God he had resented for so many decades. Over the next few days, father and daughter enjoyed warm moments together. Aggie and her husband soon had to return to America—and within a few weeks, David Flood had gone into eternity.

A few years later, the Hursts were attending a high-level evangelism conference in London, England, where a report was given from the nation of Zaire (the former Belgian Congo). The superintendent of the national church, representing some 110,000 baptized believers, spoke eloquently of the gospel's spread in his nation. Aggie went up afterward to ask him if he had ever heard of David and Svea Flood. "I am their daughter."

The man began to weep. "Yes, madam," he replied in French, his words then being translated into English. "It was Svea Flood who led me to Jesus Christ. I was the boy who brought food to your parents before you were born. In fact, to this day your mother's grave and her memory are honored by all of us."

He embraced her in a long, sobbing hug. Then he continued, "You must come to Africa to see, because your mother is the most famous person in our history."

In time, Aggie Hurst and her husband travelled there. They were welcomed by cheering throngs of villagers. She even met the man who so many years before, when she was less than a month old, had been hired by her father to carry her down the mountain in a soft bark hammock. The most dramatic moment came when the pastor escorted Aggie to see her mother's grave, marked with a white cross. She knelt in the soil of Africa, the place of her birth, to pray and give thanks. Later that day, in the church service, the pastor read from John 12:24: "I tell you the truth, unless a kernel of wheat falls to the ground and dies, it remains only a single seed. But if it dies, it produces many seeds."[13]

You will rarely read of a more heart-wrenching story of unspeakable tragedy and heartache. But what appeared to be wasted seed falling to hardened earth yielded a magnificent harvest of joy with an eternal lifespan. No matter how bad a hand life deals us or how bleak our circumstances may appear to be, we can find the strength to continue standing when we know that God is standing beside us.

When you face struggles and get handed what you don't deserve, you will be tempted to give up and give in. You will be tempted to throw in the towel. In these moments, you must make a decision either to assume God is absent and you're on your own or to believe God is present and standing beside you. The choice you make will determine whether you stand or fall. Before you choose, remember this: God is with you even when there is no evidence that He is.

. . . .

Winning Strategy 3:
Remember That You Do Not Stand Alone.

. . . .

5

When Life Seems Impossible

"Ability can take you to the top,
but it takes character to keep you there."

ZIG ZIGLAR

When I was younger, I dreamed of doing something no one in my family had ever done before—get a college degree. My father was a typical Southern patriarch; he put food on the table and worked with his hands. If something needed to be fixed, his tools were ready for use. If one of us kids were misbehaving, his weathered leather belt was always within reach. He was an honorable man and a hard worker. But he never went beyond high school.

Dad was smart, made good grades in school, and wanted to go to medical school. Unfortunately, he was raised by an unloving, uncaring, hypercritical mother and a wimpish father, which proved to be a toxic antidote to any self-confidence Dad may have had. My grandmother lived to be ninety-nine years old and never once told him she loved him. Out of six children, she made clear that Dad was the least favored. She constantly reminded him that since he was raised on a farm, with little income and little hope, he should dream only little dreams. So Dad never acquired the where-there's-a-will-there's-a-way mindset of many of his contemporaries.

Even if he'd had a different mother, there is no assurance he would have made it to medical school. Raised during the Great Depression when few boys could afford the luxury of going to college, Dad ended up working menial jobs with little income, less savings, and no pension or retirement. His résumé consisted of cotton millworker, car salesman, gas truck driver, and finally, custodian at a junior college. His main responsibility was watching the women's and men's basketball teams practice and attend to their needs (his favorite job of all, he would later say). I wonder now, years after his death, how much he mourned never having the opportunity to pursue his dream of being a physician.

Since the age of 5 (yes, 5) I decided I wanted to travel a different path. I wanted to become a lawyer. In my young mind, this would be not only a big personal accomplishment, but it would also validate that my father hadn't spent years working hard for nothing. Plus, I had watched enough lawyers on television by this time (think Perry Mason) to think that being a lawyer would be a way both to use my brain *and* make lots of money.

As I grew older, I observed how kids from wealthier families lived. I wanted to wear name-brand clothing, drive nice cars, and live in expensive homes too. My dad drove a gas truck for a living, and the most money he ever made was a hundred dollars a week. We used to plant, pick, and sell strawberries just to make enough money to go to Florida for vacation. This was hard work and not the kind I particularly enjoyed. With respect to Dad, I wanted to live better and go higher.

Defining Success

Before I graduated from high school, my mind was made up. I knew what success looked like, and I was going to grasp it with both hands. After some careful thought and some serious envy of some of my better-off spoiled friends, I defined success as:

1. Being a multimillionaire by the time I was forty

2. Living in a million dollar home

3. Being in the top 5 percent of the highest paid attorneys in the state of Georgia

4. Owning a second house on the lake

5. Being married to a beautiful woman

I went off to college, finished a degree in accounting, and was accepted to law school at a top-tier institution. But then God ruined all my plans. He nurtured a restlessness inside of me that I was supposed to do something else. As time drifted on, I recognized my call to Christian ministry. I never achieved all of my five points of success—although I knocked the ball out of the park on the fifth one—but I learned later that my list didn't make for a very good definition of success anyway.

How would you define success? Fancy possessions and clothing? A big bank balance? An expensive car and house? A corner office with a view?

I heard a story about three business professionals who were comparing ideas of what it meant to be successful. One man said, "I think I would be considered successful if I were summoned to the White House for a private, personal meeting with the president of the United States." The second man said, "To me, success would mean meeting with the president in the Oval Office, having the hotline ring during our talk, and watching the president ignore it." The third person said, "To me, success would be meeting with the president in the Oval Office, the hotline rings, and he picks it up and says, 'It's for you.'" Each man defined success differently. Maybe the last guy really had it all figured out.

I have finally reached the conclusion that much of what the world calls success is really failure in disguise. Many of you may remember the famous tennis player Boris Becker, who reportedly once contemplated suicide because of the sheer emptiness he experienced in life. Even though he appeared to be successful, he knew

> Much of what the world calls success is really failure in disguise.

his life wasn't all that it was cracked up to be. "I had won Wimbledon twice before, once as the youngest player," he said. "I was rich. Had all the material possessions I needed: money, cars, women, everything...I know this is a cliché. It is the old song of the movie and pop stars who commit suicide. They have everything and yet they are so unhappy...I had no inner peace. I was a puppet on a string."[1]

Our materialistic culture thrives on success with gurus constantly telling us how to define it and what to do to achieve it. If you go to Amazon.com, you'll find over seventy-five hundred books on how to be successful. Everybody wants to know the secret of success.

Two men were talking and one said, "Do you know the secret of success?"

"No. What is it?" the other man said.

"I can't tell you."

"Why?"

"Because it's a secret!"

Well, I can let you in on at least part of the secret of success: successfully navigating tough times. Success either lives or dies in these seemingly impossible moments. Any successful person will tell you that the deposits you make during hard times determine the withdrawals you make later. If we want to guarantee failure, then we will ignore stormy seas just to get to still waters.

Everybody craves success. Nobody wants to be known as a failure. Interestingly, the Bible talks a great deal about success. God wants you to find success in life. But He wants you find it *His way*. But what can we do to gain a correct view, a right perspective of success? How do we see past the world's disguised version of success and see it as God intended it? What if God gave us a clear view of His definition of success and that became our benchmark of living?

Consider high-definition television (HDTV). It's all the rage these days. Now when we watch Monday Night Football, we can almost count the blades of grass. In technical terms, HDTV screens contain far more lines of resolution than conventional TV screens. Digital technology has made possible the addition of hundreds of lines of resolution on a screen so that the picture is virtually lifelike.

This television innovation brings what the industry calls "super clarity." Whether you stand ten feet away or two feet away, the picture looks perfectly clear—no fuzzy lines, no distortions, and no shadows. As I work on this chapter, I'm catching bits and pieces of a golf tournament on television. I can actually slow the picture down and see the club number this golfer chose.

What would a successful life look like in high definition? What if you went from conventional living to high-definition living? What if we viewed success with razor-sharp clarity? How could that new perspective reshape the way we live our lives?

In order to find that level of clarity, we need to dig into God's Word a bit and find out what He thinks about success. I know that God wants us to find success because He said as much to a man named Joshua thousands of years ago. Joshua was about to follow the most successful leader in history to that moment, a legend named Moses. No one wants to succeed in failing to follow a success. But in order to be successful, one must understand what true success is or else failure will be the result.

Prepping for Success

A quick review of this story will put it into perspective. For four hundred years, the nation of Israel lived in bondage to Egypt. God miraculously delivered them from that bondage and promised to take them to Canaan, the land He had promised Abraham to give to him and his descendants.[2] Unfortunately, Israel disobeyed God and wandered around in the wilderness for almost forty years. But it was now time for God to fulfill His promise and for Israel to claim the land of promise God had given to them. Everything that God accomplished for Israel in the past was to prepare them for the present and for the future.

Joshua was the man responsible for making this happen and for making sure God's promise would be kept. God taught Joshua a lesson then that He is going to teach us now: Real success can be given only by God.

> After the death of Moses the servant of the LORD, the LORD said to Joshua son of Nun, Moses' aide: "Moses my servant is dead. Now then, you and all these people, get ready to cross the Jordan River into the land I am about to give to them—to the Israelites."[3]

Joshua knew that Moses was dead, and Israel knew it too. So why did God remind him? Because Joshua wasn't just following a leader; he was following a legend. Moses had been Israel's security blanket for forty years. No wonder! He was the quintessential go-to guy. He led an entire nation out of four hundred years of captivity in a single night. He parted a sea with the wave of a stick. He prayed and God rained down bread from heaven each day. When the nation was about to die of thirst, he struck a rock and water filled canteens. By any standard of measurement, Moses was a massive success.

But why? Was it his ingenuity? His creativity? His genius? No—it was the presence of God in his life.

But Moses is gone now, and for Joshua, that was bad news. But the good news was that God remained. "No one will be able to stand against you all the days of your life. As I was with Moses, so I will be with you; I will never leave you nor forsake you,"[4] God says.

You could hear Joshua's sigh of relief all the way back to Egypt! Joshua would enjoy God's constant, continuous presence the same way Moses had. What a promise! What a great reminder for you and me that there is no true, lasting, meaningful success apart from God.

Someone once said, "In whatever man does without God, he must fail miserably or succeed more miserably." Do you know why that statement is true? Because without God, all success ends in failure.

Take someone with the combined qualities of Bill Gates, Tiger Woods, Brad Pitt, and the president of the United States. You would have one of the handsomest, richest, most famous, most powerful persons in the world. This person could buy anything, go anywhere, and meet anybody he or she wants. But if they lack the presence of God—no connection to the Creator at all—they spend their days making a living but not making a life. This person might live in a mansion on a hill but not have a clue about the One who owns "the cattle on a thousand hills."[5] This person might drive a Mercedes but not be driven by the One who said, "apart from me you can do nothing."[6] This person might have more money than he could spend in ten lifetimes but not be ready to stand before the One who said, "Whoever stores up things for themselves but is not rich toward God"[7] is a fool.

Would this person be considered successful? God would say no. Jesus said, "What good is it for someone to gain the whole world, yet forfeit their soul?"[8] At death, your fame or your fortune, your wealth or your worth, will not matter. The only thing of any eternal value will be your answer to this question: Did I live my life in the presence of God and for His purpose? "He who has God and everything," said C.S. Lewis, "has no more than the man who has God alone."

Joshua had good reason to cower in intimidation. After all, he was trying to follow a legend. But God made the same promise He made to Moses because He wanted Joshua to understand that it's not the size of the man in the fight. It's the size of the God in the man. In essence, God's message to Joshua was: "I am enough for your success." God alone is the reason we are able to face tough times—a battle not only worth fighting, but a winnable battle with God.

When life seems impossible, remember that the same God who promised His presence to Joshua extends His presence to you. God's promises remain true for you just as they were for Moses and Joshua. Just as God remained with Moses and Joshua, He will remain with you if you have a personal relationship with Him.

God stays with you wherever you go. That should incite you to go anywhere God tells you to go. When God says go, He's not *sending* you somewhere; He's *taking* you somewhere.

I read a story about a boy who was afraid of the dark, and his mother asked him to go out one night to the back porch and get the mop. He didn't want to go because he was afraid. She said, "Son, haven't I always told you there's nothing to be afraid of in the darkness?"

"Yes, ma'am, but please don't make me go get that mop," he said.

"Son, don't you know that Jesus is always with you? Don't you know that you are never alone? Don't you know that you have nothing to be afraid of?"

"Yes, ma'am."

"All right, go out and get the mop," his mother said.

He opened the back door about two inches, stuck his hand out, and whimpered, "Jesus, would You please hand me that mop?"

My youngest son is a pilot for a private company that charters planes. He has to be ready to fly on a moment's notice. He doesn't get to pick the weather or the flying conditions. Every time he's called out to fly, I pray with him and my prayer always goes something like this, "Lord, put angels on each wing to protect him. I release him to You knowing that whether on the ground or in the air, You are with him." It's that realization that keeps me calm and at peace when he's flying on difficult days. The same is true for us as we fly through our own lives—whether we fly through turbulence or silky skies.

Follow the Instructions

Books on success flood the bookstores and Internet, and most are based on human wisdom and human opinion. Yet in the grand scheme of things, one sentence from God on success carries more weight and worth than a library full of human tomes. Not only has God given us a manual for real success, but He has tied success to the manual itself.

> "Keep this Book of the Law always on your lips; meditate on it day and night, so that you may be careful to do everything written in it. Then you will be prosperous and successful."[9]

God views success as simple to achieve and equally simple for Him to measure. If we are going to succeed in the things that really matter, we must follow the instructions for life found in Scripture. Now the picture grows clearer. Joshua realized he didn't need Moses. He possessed what Moses did: the presence of God to guard him and the principles of God to guide him. He would never have cause to doubt what he needed to do in crucial situations because God's Word would tell him. God gives us guidelines to greatness divinely defined.

First, we have to *look it up*. "Keep this Book of the Law always on your lips." God gives Joshua the American Express pitch about His Word: "Don't leave home without it!" In other words, success entails making a study of God's Word a constant part of your life.

I realize this will mean a radical change for many of you, because even though 93 percent of Americans own a Bible, 50 percent never read it, including 23 percent of all followers of Christ. Only 18 percent of Christ followers read the Bible every day and 57 percent do not read the Bible other than when they are at church. In fact, 10 percent of Americans think that Noah's wife was Joan of Arc![10]

No wonder difficulties destroy so many of us. If the Bible is God's manual for success, then the only way to know how to be successful is to know what God says about success. And the first thing you have to do is *look it up*. If you find the door of success closed, maybe it's because you've failed to consult God's success manual.

Next, we have to *let it in*. "Keep this Book of the Law always on your lips; meditate on it day and night." The word *meditate* refers to a cow chewing its cud, which a cow does over and over and over. So we begin by reading God's Word, but our interaction with it doesn't end there. We should think about what we've read, meditate on it, run it around in our mind. We should let it become so much a part of our heart that, as we think about life, we think about it from God's viewpoint.

I often get into tricky situations only to have a verse I meditated on come back to my mind, bailing me out of a bad decision. For example, many times I have thought about the verse,

> Even fools are thought wise if they keep silent, and discerning if they hold their tongues.[11]

That is, you never have to apologize for something you don't say. One of the best things I have ever done with my teeth is bite my lips! Some of my greatest successes in life have come from successfully failing to say anything.

After we look it up and let it in, then we must *let it out.* "Keep this Book of the Law always on your lips; meditate on it day and night, so that you may be careful to do everything written in it. Then you will be prosperous and successful."

Yes, read the Bible, study the Bible, meditate on the Bible, and even memorize the Bible. But if you want to find success in life, you must obey the Bible. You must translate truth into action.

May I tell you when God really comes alive? When you do what He wants you to do in a given situation, knowing it brings a smile to His face. When I follow the instructions, obey God, and follow His will, I know in His eyes I have been successful. No one can guarantee you success except God—and that guarantee is found in reading, meditating on, and obeying God's Word.

Find the Purpose for Your Tough Times

The greatest discovery a person can ever make is knowing why he was created. The greatest tragedy is for someone to live their life and die without ever knowing why they were created. Value and worth are directly related to purpose. A car that won't run is worthless. A pen that won't write is useless. Likewise, if we are going to be what we need to be, we need to find our purpose in life and fulfill it.

God gave Joshua his directive in life. He said, "Be strong and courageous, because you will lead these people to inherit the land I swore to their ancestors to give them."[12] Joshua received his marching orders for life from God. He knew his purpose.

Have you ever thought about the fact that there are only three types of people, and you are one of those three? First, some people live according to *no life-purpose.* They're life-drifters, aimlessly cruising through life. They go to school, get a job, switch jobs,

> Success has nothing to do with prosperity, popularity, power, or possessions. Success has everything to do with purpose.

find a spouse, switch spouses, move from house to house, place to place, retire, and eventually die. They don't *really* live. They just exist.

Then there are people who live according to the *wrong life-purpose*. They may be superachievers—people who have climbed the ladders of financial, political, and social success only to find the ladder was leaning against the wrong wall. They either realized too late or never realized that they missed a purposeful life that positively influenced others.

The third type of person is the one who lives according to the *right life-purpose*. They know why they were created. They know why God put them on this earth, and they are all about fulfilling that purpose.

This person dovetails nicely with my definition of success, which comes right from the lessons we've learned from Joshua: *Success is discovering what God wants you to be and do and then giving your best to being it and doing it.* That is the life that brings a smile to the face of God. That is success that lasts. Notice that success has nothing to do with prosperity, popularity, power, or possessions. Success has everything to do with purpose, because that is the only thing that brings a God-given guarantee of success.

I Am with You

Remember my definition-of-success list at the beginning of the chapter? Wow, how foolish that list looks now. I'm glad I didn't become that lawyer. I believe I would have been a good one and would have found success in the world's eyes. No doubt I would have made more and possessed more than I have now (though I'm not complaining—the Lord has been exceedingly good to me). But I know now I would have missed out on my *real purpose*, that one thing for which I was born. The rich experiences, the lifelong relationships, the tremendous friendships I enjoy today—I would have none of that had I pursued the world's version of success.

Just as I unearthed my purpose, Joshua realized his. And what followed his purpose was God's promise: "No one will be able to stand against you all the days of your life. As I was with Moses, so I will be with you; I will never leave you nor forsake you."[13]

What an encouragement. God said when you find the purpose I have for you and you give your life to doing it, you will be an irresistible force and your life an immovable object. When you live in the presence of God and obey the principles of God and fulfill the purpose of God, He guarantees success.

I love the movie *Ben-Hur*, a film that won more Academy Awards than any other movie in history. Charlton Heston, who played the hero in this movie, had to drive a chariot for his role. He was supposed to win the climactic chariot race, but there was one small problem: He was having trouble learning to drive the chariot.

He walked over to his director, William Wyler, and said, "Mr. Wyler, I can barely stay on this chariot. I can't win this race." Mr. Wyler looked at Charlton Heston and said, "Son, your job is to stay on the chariot. It is my job to make sure you win."

Every time you head to the office or walk into a pressure-packed meeting or job interview, don't stop trusting. When you make that dreaded doctor's appointment or confront a friend who has done you wrong, don't stop trusting. Stay on the chariot. Don't quit on God and don't stop trusting in Him. Your job is to obey, and God's is to make sure you win.

• •
Winning Strategy 4:
Stand on the Truth of God's Word.
• •

6

. . . .

When Life Tempts You to Sell Out

"Compromise is never anything but an ignoble truce between the duty of a man and the terror of a coward."

ANONYMOUS

Some moments in life rise to the top like foam on a root beer float. They stick out in your mind, etch your consciousness. One of those moments for me is the day I started college. I wandered the halls of century-old buildings, my only companion a feeling of utter isolation. My parents had driven away from campus just hours before, and I'd realized that I was alone for the first time. Nobody was going to tell me to clean my room, get a haircut, or dress for church. Curfews and mealtimes were a thing of the past.

This was my moment of liberation. Unbounded from constraints and free to be me. For the first time in my life, whatever was to be was up to me. For some kids, this epiphany would produce elation, but it generated fear in me. Remember *The Andy Griffith Show*? Well, I grew up as Opie Taylor. The only difference was my dad was not the sheriff. Other than that I lived an Opie kind of life. I grew up in the country, a naïve boy who preferred to stay close to home. So you can imagine the brand-new world I encountered when I started my college career.

For most college students, their debut days are filled with orientations and syllabi. But I had to take a test. It wasn't the kind of test you'd expect—no paper or pencils or multiple-choice questions—but rather a test of character. My character had been tested before, but I always had a cheat sheet. Somebody always stood by to help me, whether my parents or pastor or people who knew me. Now things were different.

The chains were off, the fences were down, now I called the shots. I would decide whether I would take a hit off the joint being passed around or go all the way with the girl from Introduction to English. The ball was in my court as to whether or not I'd hit the parties and get drunk, study, or go to church. Making the right decisions in each case costs something.

A few days into my first semester, students began hanging banners with strange letters painted on them. "It's rush week," one of them replied when I asked what they meant. Rush week is the equivalent of recruiting season in college football. Students attempt to show off their best attributes to fraternities and sororities in hopes of being picked by at least one. There I was, barely adjusting to not being tucked in bed by my mom, wondering if I needed to participate. Several friends and classmates encouraged me to feel it out, giving the fraternities a chance to see if they liked me and if I was interested in them. Though the whole process seemed a bit strange, I accepted an invitation to drop by one of the frat houses on a Friday night.

Keep in mind that I was Opie, even though I had already acquired the affectionate nickname "Gomer" after the Gomer Pyle character on the aforementioned show. Everyone I met acknowledged my fresh face and clean-cut innocence, a gift from my hometown of Oakwood. When I walked into the fraternity house, you can imagine the shock on my face. In the middle of the room sat a giant metal keg with enough beer to float Noah's Ark. Music was blaring, students were staggering, and what was happening on couches between guys and girls in full view—well, let's just say you wouldn't want your mother to witness it.

My heart began to pound as my feet backpedaled toward the door. A siren in my head began to bleat, and I knew I was about to make one of the greatest decisions of my life. It didn't take long. I turned to my friend: "Uh…this isn't for me." And I was gone.

> In life, we're often tempted to sell out, to give up who we're called to be, in exchange for an identity that someone else superimposes on us.

I'm not condemning drinking or joining fraternities—some of my best friends in college did both—but I realized that joining this society would mean giving up who I was. In life, we're often tempted to sell out, to give up who we're called to be, in exchange for an identity that someone else superimposes on us. During these moments, we are faced with a decision to stand comfortable in our skin or begin a long journey of trying to live up to others' expectations for us.

An Unlikely Draft

Twenty-six hundred years earlier, a young man who wasn't far from the age of most college students faced a similar situation. Unlike many high school seniors who are infatuated with graduation and can't wait to get out of the house and spread their wings, Daniel was forced out of the nest. Like many other Israelites, he was compelled to move to Babylon, a strange land that didn't observe the customs he knew from back home. There he faced a tough and unexpected test.

In the third year of the reign of Jehoiakim king of
Judah, Nebuchadnezzar king of Babylon came to
Jerusalem and besieged it. And the Lord delivered
Jehoiakim king of Judah into his hand, along with
some of the articles from the temple of God. These
he carried off to the temple of his god in Babylonia
and put in the treasure house of his god.[1]

The year was around 605 BC. God had warned the kingdom
of Judah repeatedly that if they refused to follow, worship, and
obey Him, then He would deliver them into the hands of a foreign
country. Unfortunately, Judah kept their end of the bargain and so
did God. The Babylonian army conquered Israel and captured the
capital city, Jerusalem. Babylonian King Nebuchadnezzar spear-
headed the invasion and conquest.

Nebuchadnezzar was a pagan king who reigned supreme over
a pagan country. He constructed a temple for his god, whose name
was Marduk. But every time Babylon conquered another nation,
he carried back the idols that land worshipped. He was a "god
collector," if you will. Upon returning home, he would place these
pagan gods inside his god museum.

His conquest of Israel brought with it a certain disappointment. Since Israel did not worship idols, there was nothing there
for him to confiscate. So he took some of the articles and uten-
sils that he found in the temple. But Nebuchadnezzar also had
another practice. Not only would he steal idols, but he would
kidnap individuals.

Then the king ordered Ashpenaz, chief of his court
officials, to bring into the king's service some of
the Israelites from the royal family and the nobil-
ity—young men without any physical defect, handsome, showing aptitude for every kind of learning,
well informed, quick to understand, and qualified to

serve in the king's palace. He was to teach them the language and literature of the Babylonians.[2]

Nebuchadnezzar had a brilliant idea to snatch the best and the brightest young adults and bring them back to his homeland. King Nebuchadnezzar was looking for the first-round draft picks, and he found plenty in Jerusalem—strong, youthful, handsome, brilliant. The best that Judah had to offer. Once these men arrived in Babylon, they found themselves to be a personal cog in a piece of powerful machinery.

> The king assigned them a daily amount of food and wine from the king's table. They were to be trained for three years, and after that they were to enter the king's service.
>
> Among those who were chosen were some from Judah: Daniel, Hananiah, Mishael and Azariah. The chief official gave them new names: to Daniel, the name Belteshazzar; to Hananiah, Shadrach; to Mishael, Meshach; and to Azariah, Abednego.[3]

These young men were enrolled in Babylon University. BU was the Harvard of that part of the world. Here they would receive not just education, but also a healthy dose of indoctrination. Not only was Nebuchadnezzar going to train their minds; he wanted to change their hearts. He wanted everything about them to scream "Made in Babylon." The books these young men read, the clothes they wore, the language they spoke, and even the names they were given reflected Babylonian thinking, philosophy, and culture.

Sadly, our modern world often parallels this machinery. Many colleges and universities will try to make young people forget what they've learned from their parents or their church. They want them to forget all the things they've been told were right and wrong, and they want to change them until everything about them says

"Made in _____." So often we send our children off to college and they return, hardly recognizable to us.

Studying in the world's universities is a good thing. Wearing the world's clothes, participating in the world's culture, listening to the world's music—these are all positive acts if done rightly. But often a line must be drawn in the sand when the forces around you want to reconstitute the core of who you are. Young Daniel realized this. "But Daniel resolved not to defile himself with the royal food and wine, and he asked the chief official for permission not to defile himself this way."[4]

When Daniel was asked to eat the royal food and to drink the king's wine, a trip wire was crossed. Something about this educational setup forced Daniel to draw a line, to make a decision, and to say "No!"

What was the problem? What was wrong with eating the best food in the country? Most people lived on a meager diet. Daniel was going to have the opportunity to eat, literally, like a king—the best meat, the best wine, and the best food. Why the hard line?

When you dig down into the cultural realities of the situation, more seems to be at stake. A Babylonian feast was always eaten in honor of the gods, so whenever you sat down to eat a meal, it wasn't just dining that you participated in but an act of worship. The food Daniel and his friends were expected to eat had been previously sacrificed to a pagan god. For a Jewish teenager who took his faith in God seriously, participation would mean compromising who he was called to be. By eating their meal, he would be worshipping their god.

For Daniel, reading Babylonian books and talking Babylonian language and dressing in Babylonian clothes wasn't a big deal. But worshipping the Babylonian gods was a bridge too far. This was about compromising his character, and that he would not do.

A Serious Faith

Daniel had many good reasons to say yes. He was on his own and could do as he pleased. No one would slap his hand or reprimand him. The food was great too. Steak tastes great, even when it has been sacrificed to a pagan god. Furthermore, nobody back home would ever know it. Everybody else was going to eat it. Plus, if he didn't eat it, he would be insulting the king. He wouldn't be very popular with his friends, and he might even lose his life. Daniel wasn't short on reasons to eat the food.

But he knew that God's Word was clear: Don't have any other gods before Me. Daniel's faith forbade him from doing anything that appeared to be worshipping an idol. In this scenario, then, Daniel applied a lesson in his life that protected, preserved, promoted, and prospered him in unthinkable ways: *When God says no, I say no.*

We're often faced with questions in life that leave us stranded and straining, and yet God has already given a clear answer: no. Not no like an authoritarian parent who smothers his children, but rather like a loving father who sees the danger that will be averted by avoiding the trap altogether. If you have children, you know exactly the kind of no I'm speaking about. When you tell your children to stay away from the stove, you aren't trying to control them or keep them from having fun. You're protecting them from a nasty burn that is sure to follow contact with a hot surface. This is the way God watches over us.

Unfortunately, we don't always hear God's voice. Either He seems too distant or He doesn't appear to be saying anything, despite our prayerful pleadings. But often we don't need a special word from God to determine what is right and wrong in a given situation. Daniel didn't hear from God directly in this story. The clouds never parted, a voice reminiscent of James Earl Jones didn't boom down from heaven. Instead, Daniel answers three questions, which tell him exactly what he needs to know.

Tough times are filled with trip wires. Crossing them can mean an explosion that can cost you your job, your marriage, your family, your peace of mind, your health, your freedom, and in extreme cases your life. When you carefully study Daniel's dilemma and how he dealt with it, you see an invisible checklist he went through that helped him navigate through his tough moment safely and successfully. It's a checklist that has stood the test of time and will enable you to navigate safely rough seas that can sink your career, self-esteem, conscience, and peace of mind.

Does this defile my conscience?

When confronted with the king's food, Daniel "resolved not to defile himself." The word *resolved* literally means to "purpose in one's heart." An alarm sounded in Daniel's heart, and that bell was his conscience. We all hear this siren ring at various times in life, but unlike Daniel, we hit our inner snooze button. He listened to it, and as a result, he knew more was at stake than his appetite. This is not a matter of diet, but of dedication. The problem was not obesity but idolatry. Daniel was about to make a big choice.

I'm not promoting Jiminy Cricket theology that says, "Let your conscience be your guide." Your conscience is not always a good guide. Just because you *don't* think something is wrong, doesn't mean you *shouldn't* think something is wrong. The Bible says that your conscience can be damaged and your conscience can be burned. That is why Paul also said, "My conscience is clear, but that does not make me innocent. It is the Lord who judges me."[5] Nevertheless, the conscience question is the first you should ask when faced with a difficult decision. Rarely do you make a good choice to do something if you know doing so will take your conscience on the dreaded guilt trip.

A friend of mine used to remind me, "There is a choice you have to make in everything you do. Don't forget that the choice you make makes you." God often speaks to us through our consciences—that inner voice that gives us insight into right and wrong. The way we respond to it will shape who we become.

Don't discount the pressure Daniel faced. He faced political pressure to please the king as well as peer pressure to please his friends. Hundreds of Jewish teenagers enrolled in the Babylonian University program, but Daniel was the first and only one who spoke up at that point and said no.

Imagine the conversation that unfolded. "Come on, Daniel. A little bit of food and wine doesn't really make a difference. God knows where our hearts are. Besides, everybody's doing it."

"No. Everybody is not doing it, because I'm not," Daniel says.

"But Daniel, nobody will know," one friend counters.

"God will know, and so will I. I don't have to live with you, but I've got to live with me."

The apostle Paul said, "So I strive always to keep my conscience clear before God and man."[6] Like Paul, we should work toward a heart that is clean before God and others. A good question to ask yourself whenever you're facing a decision is, "If I do this, will I be able to sleep well tonight?" Don't learn the hard way that snoozing and snoring beats tossing and turning.

> A good question to ask yourself whenever you're facing a decision is, "If I do this, will I be able to sleep well tonight?"

Does this deny my convictions?

Daniel "resolved not to defile himself." Another way to translate *resolve* is "to set aside." There were certain things Daniel had already set aside with a "do not touch" sign. The word literally refers to a religious or a spiritual conviction. You could change Daniel's home, but you could not change Daniel's heart. You could change Daniel's name, but you could not change Daniel's nature. You could get Daniel into Babylon, but you could not get Babylon into Daniel. You could change Daniel's beliefs about some things, but you could not change his convictions.

A conviction is a decision you make before you enter a tough time. If these are etched in stone, then during the storm, you can rest on your nonnegotiables. Daniel and his three buddies were unwilling to eat this pagan food and wine. But all the other Jewish boys were. What made the difference? They were all Jews brought up to believe in God and the Hebrew Scriptures. They agreed there was a difference between right and wrong.

The difference was that even though all the young men possessed beliefs, Daniel and his friends possessed and lived by their convictions.

Holding a belief differs from having a conviction. A belief exists in your head, but a conviction seeds itself in your heart. A belief says, "I am convinced of this truth." A conviction says, "I am committed to this truth." People will argue for their beliefs, but they will die for their convictions. Beliefs can change in tough times, but not convictions. Beliefs are negotiable, convictions are not. If you change a belief, compromise a belief, or concede a belief, that doesn't necessarily affect your character. A conviction, however, should not change or be compromised regardless of the circumstance.

Daniel was now forced to decide if he was going to be a conformer or a transformer. What is the difference? Pressure controls a conformer. If you place enough pressure on them, they'll cave. If you put enough pressure on them, they *will* smoke the first joint, they *will* take the first drink, and they *will* do what everybody else is doing. Principle, on the other hand, governs a transformer.

Have you decided what your core convictions are? Have you spent good times determining what you will and won't do during hard times? If not, you need to.

When I went to college I had established some core convictions. I knew I would *not* do drugs. I would *not* have sex. I would *not*

> A belief exists in your head, but a conviction seeds itself in your heart. People will argue for their beliefs, but they will die for their convictions.

cheat. I *would* go to church. I *would* share Christ. I *would* work hard and become the best student I could be. If saying yes to something meant denying my convictions, I simply said no. And I discovered living from convictions made life a lot easier.

Does this defy God's commandments?

A fascinating phrase enters the story: "Now God."[7] That's what ultimately caused Daniel to draw the line in the sand, to take the stand and to say no in his tough time. As a Jewish boy, Daniel knew the great commandment to "Love the LORD your God with all your heart and with all your soul and with all your strength."[8] If he defiled himself with the king's food and drink, he would be saying that God was not first in his life. That he loved the approval of the king or his peers more than he loved God. Once again, he came back to the principle: *When God says no, you say no.*

Just because something passes the conscience test, and even passes your conviction test, doesn't make it right because it may not pass the commandment test. Let me give you an illustration that's so twenty-first century: sex before marriage. You may have convinced yourself in your conscience that it's all right to have sex before you are married or even outside of your marriage. Perhaps you removed this prohibition from your conviction list, convincing yourself that virginity is unrealistic or celibacy is unnecessary. At that point, it doesn't matter what you think. God's Word says that sex before marriage is wrong, and God's commandments always trump your conscience and your convictions.

If God's commandments guide your conscience and determine your convictions, then the three components of your checklist will always line up. It is like an inverted pyramid:

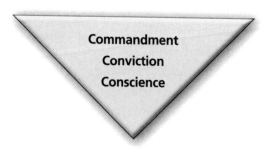

Commandment
Conviction
Conscience

The psalmist gives us words to live by: "I have hidden your word in my heart that I might not sin against you."⁹ God always has the final say. You can think something is right, you can feel something is right, and you can be convinced that something is right. But if God says it's wrong, then it's wrong. In the game of life, God's Word is always the trump card.

This may sound like God is a deity with a list of abusive rules. But He is actually a God who knows better than we do how to avoid pain, frustration, and destruction in our lives. Because He sees the edge of the cliff clearer than we do, He places guardrails next to the drop-off. Trusting that God has our best interests in mind means following His commands. And when we follow His commands, we often avoid heartache, pitfalls, and the destruction of our reputation.

Three men in the Old Testament have absolutely nothing negative said about them: Joseph, Jonathan, and Daniel. If you study the lives of all three of these men, you will find the reason they maintained such a pure and blameless life is that they answered these questions. They all three knew how to say no even when a king or a crowd said yes.

God said, "Those who honor me I will honor."[10] If you read the rest of Daniel's story, you will find that God honored him and his companions physically, mentally, and spiritually. And when you trust Him, He will honor you too.

> God knows better than we do how to avoid pain, frustration, and destruction in our lives. Because He sees the edge of the cliff clearer than we do, He places guardrails next to the drop-off.

My son Joshua took me up to fly with him for the first time a few years ago. I will never forget sitting down and hearing him tell me to buckle my seat belt. After all, I'd fastened his for much of his life. Then he began reading a checklist out loud: He was verifying that the door was closed and locked and other safety measures were being followed.

"What are you doing?" I asked.

"I'm going through my checklist. I have to do this every time I fly to make sure we're ready for takeoff."

"Let me help you do that," I said.

"No. I'll do it myself."

"Can't we just take off?" I said. "I've got work to do this afternoon, and there's no one around here."

"Nope," he said without glancing up from his sheet. "This is the way it works. Can't take you up otherwise."

There we sat on the runway, all by ourselves. Nobody else taxiing; it's just us. Suddenly, he yells out the window, "Clear!"

"Why did you do that?" I asked, a bit startled.

"You have to make sure there's nobody around the airplane before you start the propeller."

We finally took off and soared over our neighborhood. I saw roadways and hills and trees that I pass by each day, only this time from a fresh angle. I couldn't wait to get back home to tell Teresa how *we* checked the plane out together to make sure it was ready to fly. And more importantly, how our baby boy, who we had held in our arms and prayed over, now commanded a powerful plane. How life had—pardon the pun—flown by.

The true lesson from my flight that day had little to do with seat belts and propellers or even the way life passes by so rapidly. It taught me that when tough times come and tempt us to sell out, we need to make sure we respond correctly. If we trust God's checklist, when we reach the end we will be able to say, "Clear!" with confidence.

Tough times are made worse when we let little compromises slip through the cracks in our daily grind. Before you know it we're loathing the thought of our job, families, even leaving the house to spend time with friends. When we live loosey-goosey, letting our guard down, keeping the checklists in our pockets—out of sight, out of mind—we create situations and dilemmas that we might otherwise have sidestepped.

I see my checklist as a helpful guide. By God's grace I have found success in the two areas of my life that spell instant death for any pastor—women and money. I turn in receipts. I never spend church money on personal items. I never counsel women alone, dine with women alone, or visit women alone. Those are decisions made during good times that provide a pre-paved path for me to walk in during tough times. That's what knowing and sticking to your convictions can do for you.

For Daniel, it allowed him to thrive in Babylon University. For me, it gives me peace every day—knowing I am in good standing with God and my conscience is clear. It empowers me to face the most confounding decisions with confidence knowing I've won half the battle because I've looked to my conscience, my convictions, and the commands of a God who knows best.

As the Old Irish Blessing goes, when you have to take a stand and you do, and that stand is facing in God's direction, then you can be assured that the road will "rise to meet you," the wind will "be always at your back," the sun will "shine warm on your face," and the rain will "fall soft upon your fields" because God will "hold you in the palm of His hand."

Winning Strategy 5:
Make Sure You Stand Facing
in the Right Direction.

7

. . . .

When Life Says "Run"

"In any moment of decision, the best thing you can do is the right thing. The worst thing you can do is nothing."

THEODORE ROOSEVELT

Joblessness in America has soared the last several years, fluctuating between 8 and nearly 10 percent of the total workforce. Few things affect the general mood of our nation like a large number of eligible workers who can't find a job. If people are out of work, they can't provide basic necessities for their families, they risk losing their homes, and adults in the household experience profound psychological effects. I empathize with the unemployed because I used to be one.

After my post-college summer internship ended, I began searching for a job. The painful process of seeking gainful employment is something of a rite of passage for young adults, but I was facing a particularly difficult task. Our nation was in the midst of a deep economic recession, putting an end to the decades-long prosperity created by the World War II boom. America's gross domestic product was falling, gas prices were rising, and the stock market was volatile. I had graduated with a degree in accounting and had been assured by my headhunter that I was a "marketable commodity," but apparently employers weren't listening.

Months inched by without a single interview or even phone call of interest. The headhunter was growing as baffled as I, but then finally, the cloud broke and the rays of potential burst through. I landed an interview with one of the most prestigious banks in Atlanta. An entry-level employee could only dream of a position like this. The salary was more money than I'd ever seen in one place, and I was promised a fast track to a vice presidential position if I worked hard and paid my dues.

Human Resources administered a battery of emotional tests and psychological profiles, and I passed them all with flying colors. I aced both preliminary interviews and was now approaching the last hurdle to what any twenty-one-year-old would've dropped his girlfriend for. I only needed to meet with (and impress) the bank vice president who would make the final call on my hiring.

I was forewarned that I would be asked only one question, and my answer would determine my future. It required a simple yes or no response. The only problem was I was not told what the question would be. I naturally assumed it would be something along the lines of "How does four weeks of paid vacation plus a fully funded 401(k) and fat salary sound?"

Having already decided to ask for a corner office, an extended lunch break, and a stock pension plan, I brimmed with confidence. After all, the last words my headhunter said to me were, "Just give the right answer to whatever he asks you and the job is yours."

A younger man with a pleasant expression and nice demeanor greeted me at the door. He extended his hand, which I shook a bit too enthusiastically, and then led me to his office. This higher-up seemed as eager to add me to the bank's roster as I was to join it. He leaned back in a plush leather wingback and launched into casual small talk. We exchanged pleasantries. The conversation finally reached a head when he folded his hands, grinned like a Cheshire cat, leaned across the desk, and asked the question I'd been waiting for: "Is it fair to assume that your number one priority in life will be to make money for this bank and in the process make as much money for yourself as possible?"

That was not the question I was expecting. As I sat there thinking through my answer, I realized I was about to determine my career path and financial future. But most importantly, I was about to determine my number one priority in life.

I took a deep breath and told him the truth. "No sir, that would not be my number one priority. My number one priority is and always will be to glorify God with my life and to cultivate a personal relationship with Him. My family will be second, and any job I'm given will always fill the third spot." Silence permeated the room, and I felt the temperature begin to rise.

Finally, the vice president gave me a condescending look, laid down his pen, stood to his feet, and brusquely said "Thank you." Icicles hung from his words, and I shivered as he walked me out. I found out later that he was hostile to any sort of faith, and he had banned speaking of religion in his office. For him, I had committed the cardinal sin. I walked to my car with a bittersweet step. I was still unemployed with no other prospects. A sense of failure hung over my head, only trumped by the mountain of student loans that were coming due. But I also knew that I had faced a defining difficulty with honesty and courage, and this knowledge comforted me on the long ride home.

Defining Moments

All humans experience tough times, but exceptional trials define us as individuals as our responses not only determine the outcome of the situation but also the trajectory of our lives. Unfortunately, we're often unprepared for such difficulties.

I came across an interesting article titled, "178 Seconds to Live." It was about the results of twenty pilots training in a flight simulator. Each pilot was a skilled aviator but had not taken instrument training. As long as the weather was good, they were all experts in flight and had no trouble operating the plane. But when they were placed in a simulator and asked to keep their plane under control as they flew through simulated clouds and bad weather, their performance sank. All twenty pilots lost control of their planes and crashed in an average time of just 178 seconds.

> Even if life's atmosphere seems turbulence-free, you need to prepare for rough weather. Because difficulties will come.

The results showed that while they were capable of keeping the plane aloft in good weather, they couldn't survive three minutes in poor conditions.

The same is true for us. When life seems to be going our way, we are adept at making decisions and managing hiccups. But when conditions worsen, we find ourselves ill-equipped to respond and we're tempted to run away.

Even if life's atmosphere seems turbulence-free, you need to prepare for rough weather. Because difficulties will come. And often the way you respond will place you on a course that will shape the rest of your life. Winston Churchill put it in his inimitable way:

> There comes a special moment in everyone's life, a moment for which that person was born. That special opportunity when he seizes it will fulfill his mission—a mission for which he is uniquely qualified. In that moment he finds greatness. It is his finest hour.[1]

Churchill's statement reminds me of a young woman who faced her finest hour and stood tall. If her story were not in the Bible, you would swear a screenwriter had made it up. But even

Hollywood's best would have a challenge matching the incredible drama of this story. The tale is packed with intrigue, mystery, deceit, treachery, murder, romance, and a "you're not going to believe how this movie ends" conclusion.

The way Hadassah[2] handled her defining difficulty is still celebrated by Jews the world over. The Jewish calendar is constructed around three major holidays. During Passover the Jews celebrate the deliverance from Egypt, the exodus from bondage to freedom led by Moses. During Hanukkah they remember the victory of Judas Maccabaeus over the Syrians and the restoration of the temple, which is very important to Jewish tradition. But perhaps the least known celebration is the Feast of Purim. This celebration commemorates how this incredible woman faced a tough time and, when the dust settled, remained standing. During this feast Jews assemble in synagogues where her story is read publicly. Then they feast, exchange gifts, and rejoice at what this magnificent lady did.

You probably don't recognize her birth name, but you may recognize her given name: Esther. Though her language and culture are separated from ours, the lessons she teaches us are hot biscuits fresh out of the oven. I wish I could meet her, but since her story is twenty-five hundred years old, that's not going to happen. But thankfully we read about her in the book that bears her name. And because of the way she handled adversity in her life, a king did a 180 degree about-face, issued a new edict, and millions of people in 127 different countries had their lives spared.

King for a Day, Queen for an Hour

The domain of King Ahasuerus, better known by his Greek name Xerxes, stretched from modern day India to Ethiopia. He ruled over what is now known as the Medo-Persian empire, which at that time was the most revered on earth. This made Xerxes the most powerful man alive.

But power does not always translate into good decision-making. In fact, it often seduces us onto paths of destruction and failure. When it came to choosing wives and right-hand men, you could write "fail" across Xerxes's résumé. Not much is known about his queen, Vashti. We know only that she refused to submit to the king's request that she attend a banquet and display her beauty. She sends word back to the king, "Go take a hike." Saying no to a man of such power? Big no-no. She is deposed, and suddenly a large vacancy has occurred in the palace.

Realizing that not just any woman will do, the king's advisors put on a national "Miss Persia Contest," and a Jew by the name of Mordecai enters Esther into the contest, telling her to keep her Jewishness a secret since obviously no Jewish woman would ever be allowed to become a Persian queen. Amazingly, against all odds she wins, and in one day she goes from the outhouse to the penthouse. Unbeknownst to her, her coronation was God's preparation for a defining confrontation.

> After these events, King Xerxes honored Haman son of Hammedatha, the Agagite, elevating him and giving him a seat of honor higher than that of all the other nobles. All the royal officials at the king's gate knelt down and paid honor to Haman, for the king had commanded this concerning him. But Mordecai would not kneel down or pay him honor.[3]

Haman (his name sounds a little like "hangman," which is more than just a coincidence) is selected to be a trusted advisor to Xerxes. Remember, the king is not very good at choosing right-hand men. Of all the evil people described in the Bible, Haman would definitely make the top three. He is now the prime minister of one of the most powerful empires in history and has the ear of the king. He is the personification of Lord Acton's dictum, "Power tends to corrupt and absolute power corrupts absolutely."

It's not enough for Haman to have doors opened for him, to have red carpet rolled out in front of him, to eat with a silver spoon, and to hobnob with the rich and the famous; he wants everyone to bow down to him. But Mordecai is having none of it. He is a Jew, and to a Jew, bowing down to any person or thing on this earth would be considered idolatry. Haman becomes obsessed with this one moth in his Persian rug named Mordecai.

The only person in the kingdom who would not bend, who would not budge, and who certainly would not bow was this Jewish fly at his picnic. You might say that every time Haman met Mordecai on the street, it became for Mordecai a test of whether he would stand on his convictions or surrender to the pressure to compromise and save his own skin. To paraphrase, "Hell hath no fury like an ego-crazed, power-hungry prime minister scorned," and one man's vendetta is about to become a national tragedy.

> When Haman saw that Mordecai would not kneel down or pay him honor, he was enraged. Yet having learned who Mordecai's people were, he scorned the idea of killing only Mordecai. Instead Haman looked for a way to destroy all Mordecai's people, the Jews, throughout the whole kingdom of Xerxes.[4]

The current of hatred flowing through Haman's heart burst through the dam of restraint and reason and now threatens to engulf an entire nation of innocent Jewish people. Haman harbored two great hates in his heart: He hated the person Mordecai because he could not influence him, and he hated the people of Mordecai because ultimately he knew he could not influence them either.

Yet closer examination reveals a method to his madness. Haman was an Amalekite, a tribe of people who are sworn enemies of the Jews.[5] Though Haman could easily have hired some hit men to kill Mordecai, he realized if he destroyed all the Jews, he could confiscate their wealth and end up with far more money than the king would ever give him. Furthermore, his political approval rating would soar.

It appears to be the end of the line for God's people, the Jewish race. But keep one thing in mind—with God, as Yogi Berra once said, "It ain't over till it's over."

The Plot Thickens

Since Persia had recently been through a war, which depleted the treasuries of the kingdom, Haman hatches a brilliant plan. He decides to line the pockets of the king as well as his own by getting rid of the Jewish people once and for all.

> Then Haman said to King Xerxes, "There is a certain people dispersed among the peoples in all the provinces of your kingdom who keep themselves separate. Their customs are different from those of all other people, and they do not obey the king's laws; it is not in the king's best interest to tolerate them. If it pleases the king, let a decree be issued to destroy them, and I will give ten thousand talents of silver to the king's administrators for the royal treasury."
>
> So the king took his signet ring from his finger and gave it to Haman son of Hammedatha, the Agagite, the enemy of the Jews. "Keep the money," the king said to Haman, "and do with the people as you please."
>
> Then on the thirteenth day of the first month the royal secretaries were summoned. They wrote out in the script of each province and in the language of each people all Haman's orders to the king's satraps, the governors of the various provinces and the nobles of the various peoples. These were written in the name of King Xerxes himself and sealed with his own ring.[6]

Sound familiar? Haman adopts a plan that Hitler adopted two and a half millennia later. In fact, many dictators and governments have attempted the same: to marginalize, oppress, or even exterminate the Jewish people. Haman declares open season on the people of God. It will be a holocaust the likes of which the world has never seen. The king buys into this hook, line, and sinker.

> Dispatches were sent by couriers to all the king's provinces with the order to destroy, kill and annihilate all the Jews—young and old, women and children—on a single day, the thirteenth day of the twelfth month, the month of Adar, and to plunder their goods. A copy of the text of the edict was to be issued as law in every province and made known to the people of every nationality so they would be ready for that day.[7]

Talk about drama. Haman has now manipulated the signing of the death warrant of an entire nation. With one stroke of the pen, he has condemned innocent women, precious children, and little babies to untimely, undeserved death.

Only one thing stands between the Jews and complete annihilation, between evil triumphing and justice prevailing: a Jewish country girl named Esther. She is the only person who can change the mind of the king and turn the tide from tragedy to triumph. No one can pull rank over the prime minister in the court of the king except the queen. Haman may have the ear of the king, but Esther has both ears as well as his eyes.

The name *Esther* literally means "star," which seems fitting in hindsight. This defining difficulty is about to give Esther a chance to shine. Knowing this, Mordecai plays his trump card, the only card left in his hand. He tells Esther she must go to the king and plead for the life of her people. But Esther resists, knowing that if she does what Mordecai tells her to do, she will be putting her life on the line.

"All the king's officials and the people of the royal provinces know that for any man or woman who approaches the king in the inner court without being summoned the king has but one law: that they be put to death unless the king extends the gold scepter to them and spares their lives. But thirty days have passed since I was called to go to the king."[8]

No one—not even the queen—had an open door to the king. Everyone had to submit in writing a formal request to see Xerxes, and he had to respond with a formal invitation. Even then, the king had to hold out the golden scepter to show his approval or the penalty was instant execution.

Esther's moment had arrived, a reminder once again that tough times are when the greatest battles of your life are won or lost. Do you stay true to your marriage vow? Work the problem out? Fight to the finish? Or just call a divorce lawyer? Do you go through with the pregnancy? Have the baby? Or take the easy, convenient way out and condemn an innocent child to death? Do you speak up when truth is at stake? When someone's welfare is in the balance? Or do you shut up and protect your own interests? Navigating turbulence is not easy.

Esther now faces a choice. She could turn a blind eye to the peril of her people and gain the promise of safety. After all, she lived in the palace and no one knew her ethnic heritage. She was safe. But Queen Esther had another option—to rise to her destiny and risk everything to spare her people. To seize the moment and see it as her opportunity to do the right thing, say the right thing, and be the right person, live or die.

The Clock Strikes Midnight

Mordecai has enough wisdom to realize Esther faces the decision of her lifetime. If this were a movie, you would be on the edge of your seat, biting your fingernails, eyes riveted, ears perked, wanting to know what Esther will do. At this moment, Mordecai makes one of the most life-changing statements in the Bible.

> "Do not think that because you are in the king's house you alone of all the Jews will escape. For if you remain silent at this time, relief and deliverance for the Jews will arise from another place, but you and your father's family will perish. And who knows but that you have come to your royal position for such a time as this?"[9]

Mordecai pulls no punches. He reminds Esther that because of her Jewishness, she will wind up dying like everyone else. But even if she doesn't step up, God is never limited to only one option. He will raise up someone else to accomplish His purposes. Mordecai's closing question was like cold water in her face: "And who knows but that you have come to your royal position for such a time as this?"

The queen's uncle reminds her that the conundrum she faces is more than a tough decision. It's a defining moment, her finest hour. And as Mordecai hints, behind her tough time, God may be up to something. Like Esther, we often forget that sometimes adversity is a divine appointment. Behind the curtain of our difficulties, God may be up to something.

What difficulty are you staring down right now? Or better yet, what difficulty are you taking advantage of? Have you considered that you have been put in this place in this moment "for such a time as this"? You are

> We often forget that sometimes adversity is a divine appointment. Behind the curtain of our difficulties, God may be up to something.

not an accident. You are an appointment. Life is not about a coincidence; it is about providence.

Why are you here? What are the priorities of your life? Why were you born at this point in time? In this place in the world? With the abilities and giftedness that you have? Your purpose in life is never purely individualistic. The calling on your life always involves others.

In World War II, a British captive named Ernest Gordon was held in a Japanese prison camp where the POWs were forced to build a "railroad of death" for transporting Japanese troops to the battlefront. The soldiers in charge tortured and starved the prisoners while forcing them to work brutal hours on the project. More than fifteen thousand died, but somehow Gordon survived.

> Your purpose in life is never purely individualistic. The calling on your life always involves others.

After the war, he chronicled his experience in a 1962 book he called *Through the Valley of the Kwai*. He tells a story about the soldiers counting the tools at the end of a workday. Consternation rose up when a guard announced that a shovel was missing. An investigation began to uncover which prisoner had stolen it. Finally, the guard ordered that whoever was guilty must step forward and take his punishment. No one budged, and the guard grew angrier.

"All die!" the guard yelled. "All die!" He cocked his rifle and aimed it at the prisoners.

At that moment, one man lunged forward and quietly said, "I did it." The guard clubbed the prisoner to death in front of the others. In horror, his friends carried off his lifeless body while the guards recounted the shovels in the tool shed. There was no missing shovel.[10]

The man who laid down his life for his friends knew what the rest of us often forget: that God has not put any of us here solely for our own benefit, but for the benefit of others. In the family husbands and wives are to love, cherish, and enable their spouses to be the best people they can be. Parents have a primary responsibility of rearing their children to become responsible adults. In the workplace the major purpose of a boss is to enable, encourage, and equip his employees to be the best workers they can be. It really is true that no man is an island. We exist for others.

You may not be a queen in a palace or a king on a throne. Perhaps your life's locus is a school or a home or a hospital or a cubicle. Regardless, it is a sphere of influence, and you have not been placed there by random chance. You exist there to impact and influence others. When you forget yourself and risk everything for the benefit of someone else, you have the opportunity to shine like the star God created you to be.

Star Light, Star Bright

Esther realizes that Mordecai is right; she *has* come to her royal position for such a time as this. Avoiding the situation is not an option. Swallowing hard, she puts her life in God's hand and goes to the king. Esther throws a banquet for the king and invites Haman to come. The king, hardly believing that this is all she wants ("I'm sure even Esther loved to shop!"), gladly agrees.

When Haman hears of the invitation, he is excited—until he sees Mordecai once again. At the urging of his wife and friends, Haman decides to construct a gallows and, the next morning, to speak to the king about having Mordecai hanged.

But here the last and most important part of this story comes into play.

The book of Esther is different from any other book in the Bible. It is the only book where God is never mentioned. It's one of the reasons why it was almost excluded from the canon of Scripture. But I believe there is a very important reason why God Himself chose to leave His name completely out of it. You can rest assured in your life that even when you can neither see nor sense God, He is truly beside you, around you, above you, and within you.

Nothing ever happens by coincidence; it always occurs under the hand of providence. Queen Vashti's disobedience was not a mere coincidence, and neither was the king's decision to depose her. Esther becoming queen—despite the thousands of other women who competed for Miss Persia—was not a result of pure chance. God was working the whole time to light up Esther "the star" so she could shine.

After Esther has requested this banquet, the king is not able to sleep. Since his Lunesta prescription had run out, the king orders the latest royal records to be brought in and read to him. Can you think of anything more boring than reading the minutes of business meetings? Perhaps he was interested in reviewing the ledger, or maybe he thought the sheer boredom would help him finally drift into slumberland.

What does he discover? Earlier, Mordecai had overheard a plot to assassinate the king. Mordecai told Esther, who in turn informed the king. As a result, the plot was uncovered and the king's life was spared. Xerxes realizes that Mordecai has never been recognized or rewarded for his heroic act. So he calls in Haman, of all people, to ask him what he thinks should be done to honor a person the king holds in the highest regard. Haman thinks the king must be talking about him, so gladly fills up the list: "How about a Mercedes chariot, a Rolex sundial, Gucci sandals, and a diamond bracelet from Tiffany's?" The king agrees, and Haman can hardly believe his good fortune.

Reality check! The king then orders Haman to immediately go on a shopping spree, buy all the expensive stuff they have just agreed upon, and…give it to Mordecai![11] To add insult to injury, Haman even has to accompany Mordecai to the haberdashery to get him fitted for his suit, dress him, tie his shoes, and then chauffeur him around town to the cheering, adoring crowds. You're tempted to say to Haman at this point, "Cheer up. Things could be worse." And before you know it…they are.

The supernova that is Queen Esther begins to burn bright. At the banquet, she tells the king of Haman's wickedness. One of the king's attendants tells him about the brand-new gallows Haman had built, and Xerxes demands that Haman be hanged by the contraption he had constructed for Mordecai.

The king then issues an edict allowing the Jewish people to defend themselves, and the Jewish nation is spared. Mordecai moves into Haman's office, the king and Esther go away for a second honeymoon, this Jewish nation lives to see another twenty-five hundred years, and we are given a drastic reminder of just how important defining difficulties are. Not just for us but often, even though we don't realize it, for others.

We are told to shut up when we should speak up, stay out when we should walk in, or sit down when we should stand up. Esther teaches us that the cost of standing is less than the price of surrendering.

Thousands of years after Esther confronted her tough time, I faced mine in the office of that bank vice president. Looking back on that fateful morning now, I am grateful that God gave me the strength to respond rightly. Had I lied to that man or even determined to reorder my life's priorities, my trajectory would have been forever altered. I may never have met my wife, fathered my three sons, or enjoyed the company of my two grandkids. The income from that job would have made the decision to pursue seminary education difficult, and I would probably be a banker today. I imagine my alternate life, sitting in a plush office with a wallet full of money and an empty heart. I thank God that He gave me this life instead.

Never forget that God often uses what appears to be the worst to bring out the best in you. God will give you opportunities for your star to burn brightly. When He does, let yours shine.

• •

Winning Strategy 6:
Remember that the Cost of Standing Is Less than the Price of Surrendering.

• •

8

. . . .

When Life Seems to Be Against You

"Success is not measured by what you accomplish, but by the opposition you have encountered, and the courage with which you have maintained the struggle against overwhelming odds."

ORISON SWEET MARDEN

No one ever told me the word *pastor* was synonymous with *leader*. And certainly no one told me about the immense pressure or the steep price of leadership. Leaders receive blame for things they don't do, are criticized for things they try to do, and are often misquoted and misunderstood. I learned these hard lessons firsthand as a pastor.

"Other than president of the United States," said management guru Peter Drucker as he addressed a group of senior pastors from large churches, "the three most difficult jobs in America today are: president of a large university, administrator of a large general hospital, and pastor of a large church."

In my seven-year seminary experience, I learned about Greek, Hebrew, sermon preparation, and counseling. But too often pastors enter their profession ill-equipped, I think, because they never received the practical training they'll need to face the challenges of any size church. The same is true for other professions as well. Teachers learn to plan lessons and accountants learn to crunch numbers, and mechanics learn how an engine works, but they often don't learn much about leading others.

Leadership is lonely, or as Zig Ziglar says, "It's lonely at the top." If you are a leader in any venue—and most of us are whether we realize it or not—the buck not only stops at your door, but you can't move it with a bulldozer. As a leader you will hear little when things go according to plan, but when they don't go well, watch out. Leaders draw criticism as surely as a picnic draws ants.

Influencing others always comes at a price. A leader will pay the cost in time, thought, and trust. The installments look like daily risk taking, visionary thinking, diligent working, and problem solving. But the biggest cost is dealing with people, especially those who may wear the same uniform but aren't on the same team.

Jeff was a leader who served in several key areas of ministry in a church I pastored. We met for the first time at a luncheon with the pastor search committee before I had even accepted the job. I sat in a living room watching a ballgame just as they called for dinner. Before I even had a chance to get up, he blew by me, turned off the TV, and with a huff said, "Don't be rude and late." Jeff said nothing else during lunch with his mouth, but his eyes communicated he didn't care for me.

After I accepted the job, he criticized nearly everything I did and was my most vocal critic. Jeff's attitude had poisoned enough people with whom he had influence (he was a medical professional with a strong clientele and many patients in our church) that my ability to accomplish some key things was hindered if not completely compromised.

Jeff's dislike for me was so sharp that I had to confront him in a leadership meeting before twenty other men. I told him I'd had enough, and if he didn't change his tone, demeanor, and treatment of me, one of us would be leaving the church, and I was ready, willing, and able to give the church the chance to decide who that would be. To his relief, I was called to another church a few months later, and he ended up having the last word. As soon as I'd cleaned out my office, Jeff destroyed all my recorded sermons so there would be no record of my preaching there.

> Influencing others always comes at a price. But the biggest cost is dealing with people, especially those who may wear the same uniform but aren't on the same team.

Sometime after I'd left, I received word that the church was embroiled in scandal. Jeff had been caught with child pornography on his work computer. I remembered all the headaches he caused me and realized that his opposition was in some way due to the combination of my strong biblical preaching and his hidden sin. Jeff taught me that when someone on the home team seems to be batting for the opponent, you should look for the reason behind the reason. Still, nothing demoralizes and debilitates an organization or leader more than opposition from within.

Eyeing the Ball

When I read the story of Nehemiah in the Old Testament, my heart goes out to him. That man faced unreal opposition. Nehemiah tackled one of the most difficult jobs attempted by any leader in history: rebuild the walls around Jerusalem. The length of this wall was two and a half miles. Nehemiah finished it in fifty-two days. He started the project with no capital, no manpower, and no help. Initially the only enthusiasm for the project was his. Yet he completed this amazing engineering feat ahead of schedule and under budget. How did he do this? He kept his eye on the ball.

At the beginning of Nehemiah's project, the laborers who had rallied to the cause faced serious opposition. But as is the case with most projects, sooner or later all opposition finds its way to the leader because everything rises and falls on leadership (which, by the way, is the greatest lesson on leadership I have ever learned).

In football, the major goal of the defense is to pressure the quarterback into making mistakes. In war, enemies target one another's commanding officers. But even though Nehemiah's enemies aimed every single attack at him, he didn't waver. I know the feeling when you walk into a staff meeting knowing the only friend you have there is you! Working with people who either don't share your vision, don't possess a good work ethic, cause dissension, undercut your authority, or outright oppose what you do can suck the joy out of your job and the wonder out of your work.

But if we absorb the lessons this great leader teaches us, we can see difficult people as stepping-stones rather than stumbling blocks. And this will transform difficulties from miserable to magnificent.

In sports like baseball and golf, you must keep your eye on the ball. I can't tell you how many times I've both given and received the advice, "Keep your eye on the ball, Doc. Swing through." Spend any time around a Little League baseball game and you'll hear "Good eye!" echoing from the dugouts to the little batter who wisely lets a bad pitch sail by.

The same is true in marriage. Your relationship will fail if you don't keep your eye on the ball. The "ball"—your relationship with your spouse—matters most. Likewise, your business will never do what it could if you don't keep your eye on the ball and keep pressing toward the goal.

Unfortunately, staying focused is difficult. Especially when you face opposition on all sides. But this is where I draw inspiration from Nehemiah. He refused to allow difficult people to deter him from his divine purpose. And this we must also do if we're going to survive and thrive in tough times.

Keep Off the Sidetrack

Technology poses serious problems for anyone trying to focus on their to-do list or achieve even a single goal. I find myself bombarded with gadgets—from computers to smartphones to iPads—all allowing me to access the Internet at blazing speed. It's hypnotizing. It's addicting. And it's a huge distraction. I must work hard to stay focused in a world where so many people think you're not engaged if you're not getting sidetracked.

Our culture makes the concept of focus sound like an idea whose time has passed. But ask any leader of any stature and they will assure you that focus is *key* to their success. That was true for Nehemiah too:

> When word came to Sanballat, Tobiah, Geshem the Arab and the rest of our enemies that I had rebuilt the wall and not a gap was left in it—though up to that time I had not set the doors in the gates— Sanballat and Geshem sent me this message: "Come, let us meet together in one of the villages on the plain of Ono."
> But they were scheming to harm me.[1]

Sanballat, Tobiah, and Geshem were a veritable axis of evil. Up to now, they've tried to sabotage Nehemiah's wall building project with every trick in the book: derision, division, danger, and deceit. Now they try diplomacy. The three men ask Nehemiah to stop working and come talk to them.

What harm does it do to talk? he might have wondered. But then he realized that the job was not yet finished. Even though the wall was built, they still needed to hang the doors in the gates. Nehemiah recognized their request for what it was: an effort to sidetrack him from what God had called him to do. An attempt to steal his focus.

In the front of my Bible, I scribbled these words: "God wants you focused. The devil wants you finished." The biggest obstacles hindering a business from doing what it should be doing are useless meetings, silly chatter, and wasteful conversation. This verse in Proverbs comes to mind:

> All hard work brings a profit,
> but mere talk leads only to poverty.[2]

Here's the Merritt paraphrase of this verse: "Beware of the water cooler!"

We've all worked with people who would rather talk than work. Whole organizations become hobbled when they get trapped in the maze of meetings. I am well aware that some meetings are necessary, but many times we go to meetings and talk about what we should be doing rather than just getting out and doing it.

These three men didn't passively pursue this distraction. They put on the full-court press: "Four times they sent me the same message, and each time I gave them the same answer."[3] They emailed Nehemiah. They tagged him in tweets. They left messages on his mobile device. Over and over they tried to distract and detour him with dialogue. But he refused to bite. I'm sure Nehemiah's voicemail greeting sounded something like this: "You have reached the home of Nehemiah. I'm not here. I'm carrying on a great project right now. If this is Sanballat, Tobiah, or Geshem, you're wasting your time. If it's anybody else, please leave a message after the beep."

Why did Nehemiah continue working rather than shoot the breeze with these men? "I sent messengers to them with this reply:

'I am carrying on a great project and cannot go down. Why should the work stop while I leave it and go down to you?'"[4]

The phrase "great project" pulsates on the page before me. Do you know why building a wall was such a great project? *Because that was his divine purpose, the work God had called Nehemiah to do.* If you're ever going to fulfill your purpose in this life and be fulfilled in living out that purpose, you must be convinced that you're doing a great work, because it is God's work for you. Every job carries a purpose, and you must be convinced in the greatness of yours. All meaningful work is God's work and all of God's work is a great work.

> Every job carries a purpose, and you must be convinced in the greatness of yours.

I tell people in our church, if you work in the children's area teaching Bible stories to children, you are doing a great work. If you care for little babies and sing to them about Jesus, you are doing a great work. If you work with teenagers, helping them learn how to be godly adults, you are doing a great work. And the same is true for you. If you invest your gifts in being a homemaker, you're doing a great work. If you're applying your gifts and passions in the marketplace, you're doing a great work.

When distractions sidetrack us, many great works never get accomplished. Years ago an Eastern Airlines jet crashed in the Florida Everglades en route from New York to Miami. It was the infamous Flight 401, loaded with holiday passengers. As the plane approached the Miami airport, the light indicator for proper deployment of the landing gear failed. The plane flew in a large looping circle over the swamps of the Everglades while the cockpit crew checked to see if the gear truly had not deployed or if the bulb in the signal light was defective.

When the flight engineer tried to remove the signal-light assembly, it wouldn't budge. The other members of the crew tried to help him. As they struggled with the light assembly, no one noticed the aircraft was losing altitude. The plane flew right into the swamp, killing 103 people.

While an experienced crew of high-priced pilots fiddled with a six-dollar bulb, a passenger-filled jet crashed into the ground. Remember this simple lesson. The difficult people you encounter at work and in life represent the lightbulbs. You cannot allow them to deter you from the main goal.

You'll be tempted often to choose the urgent over the important in leadership. As you try to keep your eye on the ball, this dilemma will threaten your focus. "How do I choose what is best over what is merely good?" "How do I choose the long-term perspective over the short-term one?" You must not lose focus; your task is too *important.*

I heard about two old golfing buddies who were playing a water hole when one hit his shot right into the pond. As they searched around the pond for the ball, one of them ran across a talking frog.

"If you kiss me," the frog said, "I will turn into a beautiful princess."

Well, the partner heard what the frog said and was shocked when his buddy reached down, picked up the frog, and put it in his pocket. He looked at him and said, "Why didn't you kiss her?"

The old man said, "At my age, I would rather have a talking frog."

That man kept his priorities straight.

If you decide what your priorities are, your priorities will help you decide everything else. They will help you keep your eye on the ball. When life seems to be against you, ask yourself, *What are my biggest priorities for this day? For this week?* Settle those in your mind and be laser-beam focused on them as you confidently pursue the great work of your life.

Don't Listen to the Chatter

If at first you don't succeed, try, try again. That's what Sanballat, Tobiah, and Geshem did:

> Then, the fifth time, Sanballat sent his aide to me with the same message, and in his hand was an unsealed letter in which was written:
> "It is reported among the nations—and Geshem says it is true—that you and the Jews are plotting to revolt, and therefore you are building the wall. Moreover, according to these reports you are about to become their king and have even appointed prophets to make this proclamation about you in Jerusalem: 'There is a king in Judah!' Now this report will get back to the king; so come, let us meet together."[5]

When their attempts to sidetrack Nehemiah failed, his enemies resorted to slander. In those days, people wrote letters on papyrus or leather, rolled them up, tied them with a string, and then secured them with a seal of wax or clay to make sure that only the proper authority opened it. But these three guys had a devious plan. They wrote an open letter, somewhat like a letter to the editor or a petition. Today it would be like writing about it on your blog, posting it on Facebook, or sending out a tweet. They wanted everybody to read it, especially the king, who had given Nehemiah permission to rebuild the wall. If this rumor got out, it could cost Nehemiah not only the wall but his life.

They were spreading pure, unadulterated gossip, and they

wanted it in print. They knew what they were doing, because gossip in print is doubly difficult to correct.

Years ago, a typographical error occurred in a small-town newspaper's classified ads, followed by subsequent attempts to correct it:

> **Monday:** *For Sale*—R.D. Jones has one sewing machine for sale. Phone 948-0707 after 7 pm and ask for Mrs. Kelly who lives with him cheap.

> **Tuesday:** *Notice*—We regret having erred in R.D. Jones's ad yesterday. It should have read: "One sewing machine for sale, cheap. Phone 948-0707 and ask for Mrs. Kelly, who lives with him after 7 pm."

> **Wednesday:** *Notice*—R.D. Jones has informed us that he has received several annoying telephone calls because of the error we made in the classified ad yesterday. His ad stands corrected as follows: "*For Sale:* R.D. Jones has one sewing machine for sale. Cheap. Phone 948-0707 after 7 pm and ask for Mrs. Kelly who loves with him."

> **Thursday:** *Notice*—"I, R.D. Jones, have *NO* sewing machine for sale. I smashed it. Don't call 948-0707 as the telephone has been disconnected. I have not been carrying on with Mrs. Kelly. Until yesterday she was my housekeeper, but she quit."[6]

If you want to ruin someone's reputation, don't just speak gossip. Place it in a public forum. Picture Nehemiah's enemies trying to pull off something similar. Today we'd call it political hardball, negative campaigning, or dirty tricks. Nehemiah faced a mudslinging campaign—a down and dirty, pulling out all the stops affront designed to destroy his integrity and his work.

One of the best pieces of advice I ever received concerning

anonymous mail comes from baseball legend Yogi Berra: "I never answer anonymous mail." While his words make us smile, they are also quite astute. I have followed that advice for over twenty-five years, never reading or responding to the charges of anonymous critics.

I love the story of the pastor who received a letter in the mail one morning and all it contained was one word in big and bold print—"FOOL!" The next Sunday he stood before his congregation, held up the letter, and said, "I received the strangest letter this past week." He read the one word text and then said, "Somebody wrote this letter and forgot to sign it!"

Ironically, Nehemiah's enemies criticized him for the very thing they were guilty of themselves. They criticized him for being power hungry, but they had the story backward. They were the ones who were drunk on power. They felt threatened and craved control. If you watch carefully, you'll notice people will often criticize in others the very trait they themselves have.

I heard about a husband who suspected his wife was losing her hearing. One night he positioned himself across the room from her as she sat in her favorite chair with her back to him. Very softly he said, "Can you hear me?"

When she didn't answer, he moved a little closer and repeated very softly, "Can you hear me?" Still no answer.

He then moved closer and again said, "Can you hear me?" Still no answer.

Finally, he got right behind her chair and said right into her ear, "Can you hear me?"

She looked him in the eye and said, "For the fourth time, yes!"

No source was given for the accusations against Nehemiah. The letter read, "It is reported among the nations." Always stand prepared when someone comes to you and says something like this: "I heard…" or "Somebody said…" or "The word on the street is…" Never receive a criticism from someone who is bring-ing it on behalf of someone else—someone they won't even name.

Not even slander could keep Nehemiah from stopping the work he was doing. I love his response. "I sent him this reply: 'Nothing like what you are saying is happening; you are just making it up out of your head.'"[7]

Nehemiah tells them to go fly a kite. "I don't care what you think. I don't care what you say. I don't care what you don't like. I'm going to keep building this wall until the job is done." His atti-tude reminds me of a lady who approached Winston Churchill one time. Lady Astor, a member of the British Parliament, was a constant thorn in his side, always critical. The two of them got into a heated conversation once and she said, "Winston, I don't like your politics and I don't like your mustache." He looked at her and said, "Madam, I see no earthly reason why you should ever come into contact with either one."

You have to approach tough times with an "I am going to give today my best shot" attitude or else they will not only beat you down, they will keep you down. At any given moment during difficult times, you're either being productive or allowing others to be destructive in your life.

Nehemiah knew what his adversaries were doing and he knew they could hurt him. He did the one thing you can always do with any critic and any criticism: take it to God.

> They were all trying to frighten us, thinking,
> "Their hands will get too weak for the work, and it
> will not be completed."
> But I prayed, "Now strengthen my hands."[8]

On my desk, I have a quote from Dwight L. Moody that says, "If I take care of my character, God will take care of my reputa-tion." If you will just stay on task, do what you know to do at any given moment, your tough times will be easier to weather.

Stand Against Seduction

One more person enters the scene and tries to take Nehemiah off that wall and away from the work. His name is Shemaiah. He was a priest and a onetime friend of Nehemiah. But someone bought him off and he tried to get Nehemiah to compromise his integrity.

> One day I went to the house of Shemaiah son of Delaiah, the son of Mehetabel, who was shut in at his home. He said, "Let us meet in the house of God, inside the temple, and let us close the temple doors, because men are coming to kill you—by night they are coming to kill you."[9]

Shemaiah wanted to make Nehemiah look like a coward, because if he cut and ran, he would lose all credibility before his people. Nehemiah was so devoted to doing what God called him to do that even if it did indeed cost him his life, he was not coming off that wall until the wall was finished. That is why he said to Shemaiah, "Should a man like me run away? Or should someone like me go into the temple to save his life? I will not go!"[10]

Difficult people are often placed in our path not to defeat us but to develop us. Leaders know this, so they refuse to run; they stay and finish the job regardless of the cost. Just as the captain goes down with the ship, the leader stays until the work is done.

Shemaiah not only wanted to make Nehemiah a coward; he wanted to make him a compromiser. The word for temple can

> Difficult people are often placed in our path not to defeat us but to develop us. Leaders know this, so they refuse to run; they stay and finish the job regardless of the cost.

also mean Holy Place or sanctuary. Shemaiah tried to tempt Nehemiah to run to the place where only the priests could enter and there try to kill him. But Nehemiah was a layman and according to Numbers 18:7, God forbade anybody except the priests to ever go into the Holy Place. Shemaiah was trying to get Nehemiah to do something that would shame him, even kill him. Nothing will kill the moral authority a person needs to lead quicker than compromise.

In the early 1970s, the Iraqi government arrested a group of American students on trumped up espionage charges. Saddam Hussein's regime demanded confessions. In order to elicit admissions of guilt, they tortured the students. The prisoners were told that if they confessed they were spies, they would go free. In other words, "Compromise the truth; admit to a lie."

The promise of freedom became irresistible. One by one, as the pressures and the pain mounted, the prisoners confessed to crimes they had not committed. Every student confessed, except one. The torture intensified for this man. The loneliness of isolation became unbearable. He came close to breaking, but he didn't.

Recounting this man's story in the *Wall Street Journal*, Mark Helprin wrote,

> Then they announced that they were finished with his case, that he could simply confess or die. A confession lay before him as they raised a pistol to his head, cocked the hammer and started the countdown. He had heard executions from his cell. "Sign your name," he was told, "and you will live," but he refused. He closed his eyes, grimaced and prepared to die. They pulled the trigger. When he heard the click, he thought he was dead. The gun however had not been loaded.[11]

That student was eventually released, but he discovered afterward that every other prisoner who had confessed was hanged in the public square. He was the only survivor. He learned a valuable lesson about facing tough times: *Compromise represents a far greater risk than courage.* In dealing with difficult people or hostile working environments, you and I will be tempted to "go along to get along." Don't do it. Compromise when feasible, confront when necessary.

Let me give you a three-part maxim for tough times that is also helpful anytime:

1. It is always right to do right.
2. It is never wrong to do right.
3. It is never right to do wrong.

Nehemiah didn't go into the Holy Place. Incidentally, how did he know that Shemaiah, who was a priest, was also a false prophet? How did he know that this idea of going to the Holy Place was not a good idea? Simple. It was contrary to God's Word. In other words, you do the right thing no matter what—whether it's a scriptural principle, a company policy, or a law on the books.

Now we get the punch line of the first half of Nehemiah's book: "So the wall was completed on the twenty-fifth of Elul, in fifty-two days."[12]

Archeologists have unearthed a part of Nehemiah's wall. It was not only two and one half miles long; it was ten feet across and twelve feet high. It was finished in fifty-two days. How would their findings vary if Nehemiah had lost focus? If he'd lost confidence in the great work he was doing? What if he'd been sidetracked by his adversaries' slander and meeting requests? Even one misstep in any of these cases and Nehemiah would have missed God's best and an entire book in the Bible would be missing. In those alternate realities, Nehemiah's name never would have been known in our time. Keeping his eye on the wall meant the difference between the life and death of his vision.

When you're facing adversity—a hostile working environment, difficult people, office politics, petty opposition—life can be downright miserable. I've been there, and it's awful. But these rapids don't have to flip our rafts. We can choose a different path. The journey will not be a cakewalk, and you can expect many obstacles. But anything worth doing will not be easy. A special beauty comes with operating within your skill set and your life's purpose—the beauty of single-mindedness, the beauty of reaching your goal though the world seems out to destroy you.

You might not have received formal leadership training in school, but you can know your purpose. You can understand the role you were called to play in your organization, in your family, in your community. Stay focused, avoid detours, resist compromise, do the right thing, and you will remain standing even when life seems to be against you.

Go build your wall!

- -
Winning Strategy 7:
Stand Focused on the Task at Hand.
- -

9

When Life Is Insufferable

*"Although the world is full of suffering,
it is also full of overcoming it."*

HELEN KELLER

I sit in snow-covered Liverpool, New York, watching the sky spit icy dust from above. On this cold blustery March morning, my mind wanders back to a funeral I preached this past Saturday for one of my neighbors. I never expected to do Big Mike's funeral. It came as a result of God working through, you guessed it, a tough time.

Mike lived around the corner and a few houses down from me. In the eleven years I have lived in the neighborhood, we had crossed paths maybe only three or four times. I'd see him at a neighborhood barbecue. We would exchange pleasantries, but each of these encounters was uneventful, if barely memorable. We first met at a neighborhood-wide mixer he was hosting. The event was BYOB, and since I was known to be a minister, Mike didn't expect me to attend.

When Teresa and I strolled up his driveway, a peculiar expression came over his face. He clumsily tried to hide his beer can next to his hip. Even though I tried to make him feel at ease, he still avoided me as if I were diseased. As a result, we barely spoke for the next decade, mostly because he was reluctant to talk with me.

Then last spring I was informed by one of my neighbors that Mike had been diagnosed with inoperable esophageal cancer. I was stunned at the diagnosis—he was a mere fifty-one years old—and saddened that I failed to reach out more than I did. I could count on one hand the conversations we'd had.

Though I could not make up for lost time, I decided to pay Mike a visit. When he met me at the door, I noticed his frame was already much smaller than I remembered from the neighborhood socials. Also unlike those gatherings, Mike seemed to want to talk this time.

After some small talk, I transitioned to weighty matters, and the dam broke. Salty tears cascaded down the sides of my face.

"Mike," I said, voice trembling, "I am not weeping because you're sick. It's because in ten years I never shared with you what I came to share today. Do you mind if we talk about spiritual things?"

Mike cleared his throat. "James, I would like that very much."

I shared how much God loves him and how Jesus Christ had radically changed the course of my life. I talked about grace and forgiveness and salvation. Mike was vacuuming every word I said into his heart, and he told me he wanted to receive Christ as his Savior and Lord. "I'm not quite sure how to do this," he said, "so would you help me?"

I walked over to the couch where he was sitting, grabbed his hand, and prayed. As a pastor, I've witnessed many conversions, but I don't know that I ever experienced a more palpable life change. We looked at each other with tears in our eyes and hugged each other like long lost brothers. I had no way of knowing that Mike and I were starting down an eight-month journey together.

I visited him several times every month. Each visit marked another decline in his health. A once strapping man of 220 pounds had fallen to less than 100. But while he was physically wasting away, he was spiritually soaring. I'd recommend verses to read in the Bible I gave him, and the next time I walked in the door, he would proudly show all he'd highlighted and ask for a new list. The bitterness Mike harbored about having a terminal illness at such a young age melted away. His wife couldn't believe the change in his demeanor, countenance, and attitude. He was still battling, but now he lived with the promise of eternal life, and if he didn't make it, he would be with Christ in heaven.

Not long before he died, I dropped by to visit Mike on my way home from work. As we talked about his faith, he admitted to me that he was grateful for what had happened to him. I was a bit stunned. But from Mike's new perspective, cancer provided the pathway to Christ. Though he lamented that it took cancer to draw him to Christ, he insisted he wouldn't go back to his old life for anything. Mike had learned his greatest lesson not in health but in sickness, not in prospering but in suffering.

Then one morning (one week ago today as I type these words), I received the call I'd been dreading. A neighbor informed me that if I wanted to see Mike one last time, I needed to rush to his home. Unfortunately, I wasn't able to reach the house until 5:00 p.m. When I walked into his bedroom, his teary-eyed wife said, "He told me he would not die until he heard your voice one last time and that you would tell him it was okay to go."

I walked in, and when I saw his shriveled body, I wept uncontrollably. Though he was unconscious, when he heard my voice he smiled faintly to let me know he was there. I stayed for an hour, reading Scripture and praying. The time to go finally arrived, but I had one last thing to do. I returned to Mike's bedside, leaned down, and kissed his feverish forehead. With my tears falling onto his face, I whispered into his ear, "Mike, you can let go now." And he did.

Why, God?

If you could ask God one question and be guaranteed an answer, what would you ask? When pollster George Barna asked this question in a national survey, the primary response was, "Why is there pain and suffering in the world?"

I confess that in my thirty-five-year ministry, that question is far and away the number one question people ask me. And it comes in two forms: "Why do bad things happen to good people?" and "How could a loving God allow evil in the world?"

The latter question, however, assumes that a loving God and suffering cannot go together. Many of us remember one of the most famous trials in the twentieth century, the trial of O.J. Simpson. After what seemed to be an open-and-shut case with overwhelming evidence that pointed to Simpson as the murderer of his ex-wife Nicole Brown and Ron Goldman, the world watched in shock when the final sentence was handed down. Judge Lance Ito's clerk, Deidre Robertson, read the jury's verdict: "Not guilty." Nicole's mother looked up and said, "God, where are You?"

We have all either asked or heard others ask, "Why is this tragedy happening to me?" If you've never asked, "Where is God when it hurts?" you will. You may think right now this chapter does not apply to you, but you may need it during the next tough time you face or the one after that. At some point in our lives, we all face the problem of pain and suffering. The hard questions mount until we are overcome with grief. Though you may be bumping along life's path fine and dandy right now, it's a good idea to prepare for that tough time. It *will* come.

Three basic problems exist that are common to everyone, everywhere at some time in this life. They are sickness, sorrow, and suffering. That triumvirate can really make tough times miserable. You may escape one or even two of these, but you will never escape all three.

Even the godliest of people are not exempt from pain and suffering. One of the greatest Christians of all, the apostle Paul, knew what it was to have problems. In fact, Paul closes the eleventh chapter of 2 Corinthians telling readers how he had been whipped, shipwrecked, robbed, mugged, betrayed, jailed, and left for dead. His highway of holiness was not paved with rose petals; it was paved with hurt, heartache, and hardship.

Then in chapter twelve, Paul mentions a problem that was so difficult, so painful, so debilitating that even with his great faith, he found himself asking, "Where is God when it hurts?" Paul experienced real suffering. This pain was so bad that he kept it a secret for fourteen years. No one else knew about this problem until he wrote the letter to the Corinthian church.

Paul's pain was no passing ailment. We don't know what it was, but we do know that Paul hurt and he hurt badly. It was through his pain and his suffering that God taught him some of the greatest lessons of his life and ministry.

Many great thinkers and theologians, including C.S. Lewis, have written about pain and suffering. I'm not trying to top what these writers have said, but I do want to add my own view and expand on the truths that so many have communicated so well over the years. What follows are a few of the lessons I've learned through the life of Paul and how he dealt with his own tough times. Though he was familiar with suffering, Paul was a man of strong faith. It makes sense to plumb the depths of his experience and see what his testimony can teach us about our own pain and suffering.

We Are Not Alone

Tough times can be grueling, but worse than the suffering itself is the sense of isolation it brings. You survey those around you who aren't experiencing your pain or you find yourself in a community where everyone else seems to be thriving, and your experience makes you feel cut off from others. No matter how many good friends or counselors you may have, tough times can still bring remoteness and seclusion into your life. But one of the most comforting truths you can experience in these moments is the assurance that even when you feel lonely, you are not alone. If we dig into Paul's second letter to the Corinthian church, we find this idea prominently displayed.

In the first several verses of chapter twelve, Paul speaks of an unbelievable experience God gave him. He'd seen things that no other person had seen and reached great heights in his spiritual life. On the heels of that great experience, however, God did something else: "So to keep me from becoming conceited because of the surpassing greatness of the revelations, a thorn was given me in the flesh."[1]

The phrase "thorn in the flesh" is one of the most famous in the Bible. We get the expression "a thorn in my side" from it. Theologians and Bible scholars still debate exactly what Paul meant by this. Some say it was poor eyesight and others a speech impediment. Some claim it was a physical handicap and still others his mother-in-law. Okay, I'm just kidding about the last one, but you get the point. We don't know what this thorn was because we're not specifically told.

I believe there's a reason God obscures these details from us. After all, the Holy Spirit could have inspired Paul to use more specific language, but He doesn't. God seems to hide the meaning of this metaphor because the truth of the passage transcends any specific malady. If this problem had been poor eyesight, then many people would say, "Well, that doesn't help me because I have twenty-twenty vision." If Paul's ailment had been a speech impediment, then those of us with the gift of communication would not find comfort in his words. God placed the anonymous thorn in this text because no matter what your particular affliction might be, the same God that gave Paul victory over his thorn can give you victory over yours. What a comforting thought.

We don't have to debate *why* this thorn had come into Paul's life. He tells us twice that it was to keep him "from becoming conceited" or proud. Have you ever noticed that when life is going great, staying close to God is difficult? We tend to think that life is great because we are so great, that God is so good to us because we are so good to Him. We must always guard against becoming too big for our spiritual britches.

I love how God can use anything both for good and for His glory. In His wisdom and patience, He does something for us that we think is intended to hurt us. But then God turns it around and it helps us. Here is what He does: *He balances blessings with burdens.*

God gives us daily blessings, even those of us without financial riches or a thriving marriage or physical health. Just being alive means we've been blessed with the gift of today. The psalmist reminds us that God blesses us each day: "Blessed be the Lord, who daily loads us with benefits."[2] But just as our Creator fills our hands with blessings, He often also places burdens on our back.

> One of three things must be true of you: Either you are in the midst of a storm, you are coming out of a storm, or you are about to sail into a storm.

Tough times are one of life's inescapable realities. When my kids were growing up, I'd often remind them, "One of three things must be true of you: Either you are in the midst of a storm, you are coming out of a storm, or you are about to sail into a storm."

These words were intended to set reasonable expectations about life's pains and harshness.

But why does God give (or at least allow) burdens? If God filled your hands only with blessings, eventually you would fall on your face. Likewise, if He continuously loaded your back with burdens, you would fall on your hindquarters. So the Lord perfectly balances blessings and burdens so that we don't become imbalanced.

We find this same kind of balancing act in Jesus Christ's life and ministry. He experienced many blessings during His life: miracles, friendship, ministerial successes. Yet He also bore the burden for our sins. Just look at the cross—God suffers *for* us, but He also suffers *with* us. The life, death, and resurrection of Jesus give me great confidence that God stands with us in our pain and suffering.

In 2000, I was elected president of the largest Protestant denomination in America. I still don't fully understand why the people of the Southern Baptist Convention (SBC) afforded me such an honor, but I am grateful. Every SBC president determines early on what they want their legacy to be, and my evangelist heart turned toward the mission field. I determined to use my terms of service to visit every region of the world (all fourteen of them) and encourage our SBC missionaries serving there.

Toward the end of my second term in 2002, I was in Cambodia. My legs ached, my body suffered from severe jet lag, and I missed my family. My missionary host took me to visit a Buddhist temple in the area so I could see where the local residents worship. Walking into the stacked stone building, I encountered a massive statue of the Buddha. Incense offerings filled my nostrils as I surveyed his portly frame: crossed legs, folded arms, closed eyes, a slight smile creasing his face. He seemed to possess more serenity than I'd known in weeks. But he also appeared remote, totally detached from the suffering of planet earth.

With worshippers kneeling around me, my mind returned to the God I worship in Jesus. I thought about the "suffering servant" who endured agony on the cross. With these two images juxtaposed in my mind, a lightbulb came on: My God is not only *for* me but *with* me. My weary muscles and mind began to relax.

How easy we forget the great suffering and blessed work Jesus accomplished for each of us on the cross. I walked out of the temple that day with a scene from the play *The Long Silence* (author unknown) running through my mind. It encapsulates well the sentiment I was feeling as I stood in front of the Buddha statue:

> At the end of time billions of people were scattered on a great plain before God's throne. Most shrank back from the brilliant light before them, but some groups near the front talked heatedly—not with cringing shame, but with belligerence.
>
> "Can God judge us? How can He know about suffering?" snapped a pert young brunette. She ripped open a sleeve to reveal a tattooed number from a Nazi concentration camp, "We endured terror…beatings…torture…death!"
>
> In another group an African-American boy lowered his collar. "What about this?" he demanded, showing an ugly rope burn. "Lynched…for no crime, but being black!"
>
> In another crowd a pregnant school girl with sullen eyes said, "Why should I suffer, it wasn't my fault."
>
> Far out across the plains there were hundreds of such groups. Each had a complaint against God for the evil and suffering He permitted in this world. How lucky God was to live in heaven where all was sweetness and light, where there was no weeping or fear, no hunger or hatred. What did God know of all that man had been forced to endure in this world? For God leads a pretty sheltered life they said.

So each of these groups set forth their leader, chosen because he had suffered the most—a Jew, an African-American, a person from Hiroshima, a horribly deformed arthritic, and a child with Down syndrome. They consulted with each other. At last, they were ready to present their case, and it was rather clever.

Before God could be qualified to be their judge, He must endure what they endured. Their decision was that God should be sentenced to live on earth—as a man!

"Let Him be born a Jew. Let the legitimacy of His birth be doubted. Give Him work so difficult that even His family will think Him out of His mind when He tries to do it. Let Him be betrayed by His closest friends. Let Him face false charges; be tried by a prejudiced jury and convicted by a cowardly judge. Let Him be tortured.

"At the last, let Him see what it means to be terribly alone. Then let Him die. Let Him die so there can be no doubt that He died. Let there be a great host of witnesses to verify it."

As each leader announced his portion of the sentence, loud murmurs of approval went up from the throng of people assembled. When the last had finished pronouncing sentence, there was a long silence. No one uttered another word. No one moved, for suddenly all knew that God had already served His sentence.

> God understands those feelings, and rather than tell you everything will be okay, He whispers, "You are not alone."

Whenever I find myself in the middle of sickness, sorrow, or suffering, I look at the cross and remember that God stands with me in my pain.

The promise extends to you. Perhaps you feel alone as you sink in the vortex of your heartache and anguish. God understands those feelings, and rather than tell you everything will be okay, He whispers, "You are not alone. Christ walks with you." Embedding that truth into your heart and soul can stand you upright when you struggle even to lift your head.

God's Language of Suffering

Even when we don't feel alone in tough times, we may still find it hard not to respond with raw, visceral reactions. After all, we're only human. But how did Paul respond to his suffering?

"Three times I pleaded with the Lord to take it away from me."[3]

Have you ever asked God to heal you of a sickness or relieve you of a sorrow or alleviate your suffering, but He didn't do it? Well, join the club. Three times Paul didn't just pray but pleaded with God. He begged the Healer to remove this thorn, but God chose not to. There was nothing wrong with the prayer and there was nothing wrong with God. God heard Paul's plea and He cared deeply. When He finally responded, He didn't offer the answer Paul desired. But it was the answer he *needed*.

Paul wanted God to deal with his problem by subtraction, but instead God dealt with his problem by addition. The beauty in Paul's prayer comes from God extending love to His child. Right in the middle of Paul's prayer, right in the middle of his pleading, right in the middle of his hurting, right in the middle of his suffering, God spoke to Paul. "My grace is sufficient for you,"[4] God said.

The apostle didn't get the answer he was looking for until he quit praying and started listening. Sometimes we're so busy telling God what He ought to do *for* us that we can't hear God telling us what He wants to do *in* us. If you have a problem in your life, and you've asked God to take it away and He hasn't, maybe it's time for you to quit talking and start listening.

God taught Paul lessons in the best time he could learn them: during difficulties. The bad news about tough times turns out to be good news after all: You'll learn more about God and you'll learn much more from God in the valley than you will on a mountaintop. I love the way C.S. Lewis describes how God uses pain to communicate with us. "God whispers to us in our pleasures," Lewis writes, "speaks to us in our conscience, but shouts to us in our pains; it is His megaphone to rouse a deaf world."

> Suffering jars us into reality and reminds us of our mortality and frailty. But most importantly, it shifts our gaze to God.

My friend and church member Laurie emails me almost every week. Though she wrestles with terminal cancer, Laurie is one of the most radiant Christ-followers I've ever known. Her battle has dragged on for more than two years. She leapfrogs from treatment to treatment in an attempt to stay one step ahead of this relentless enemy who never flags nor falters. Last week she sent me an email asking me to pray that her liver markers would stay down and that her body would allow her to continue on this brutal regimen of chemical cocktails.

I usually dread receiving this type of correspondence, but Laurie's emails don't depress me or drag me down. They boost me up. She fills every email with praise for God's goodness, acknowledgment of His mercy and love, and gratitude for how He's used these tough times to draw her closer to Him. The thread that runs through her emails constantly reminds me that suffering jars us into reality and reminds us of our mortality and frailty. But most importantly, it shifts our gaze to God.

Pain, sorrow, and suffering act as God's chief venue to experience His grace. More than anything, God wants you to luxuriate in it *daily*. There is no grace without suffering and no grace apart from suffering. So listen in your pain. You will hear God shouting, "My grace is sufficient for you." How does God spell *relief*? G-R-A-C-E.

Our Suffering, God's Strength

Though we may not be totally at peace with it, we know life without pain does not exist. In time, we will all experience misery. But how we respond determines whether we live in victory or defeat. If your agony leads to resistance, resentment, and bitterness, then you will live a defeated life. If it leads to prayerfulness, patience, faith, and trust, then you will live a victorious life. As Paul says,

> But he said to me, "My grace is sufficient for you, for my power is made perfect in weakness." Therefore I will boast all the more gladly about my weaknesses, so that Christ's power may rest on me. That is why, for Christ's sake, I delight in weaknesses, in insults, in hardships, in persecutions, in difficulties. For when I am weak, then I am strong.[5]

Can you see how Paul has turned 180 degrees? Before God spoke, all Paul wanted was to lose his problem. After God spoke, he realized that in his problem he had found something better and greater—a supernatural strength that God reserves for those tough times when we realize His presence is greater than our problems and His purpose is bigger than our pain.

Victor Frankl, a Jewish neurologist and psychiatrist survivor of the Holocaust, who spent three years of his life in a Nazi concentration camp, said, "Suffering only has meaning provided that the suffering is unavoidable. If it is avoidable, the meaningful thing to do is to remove its cause for unnecessary suffering is masochistic rather than heroic. If on the other hand one cannot change a situation that causes his suffering, he can still choose his attitude."[6]

You can look at suffering either as an enemy to avoid, as a master to surrender to, or as a servant that God can use to minister in your life. Our weakness, remember, provides God the opportunity to show His strength.

One of my former staff members (I'll call him Sam) realized through his own affliction the lesson that God gave Paul. A few years ago, I received the most distressing correspondence from him. He woke up one morning and his arm felt asleep. It tingled all day and the next day and the next. Assuming it was a pinched nerve, he visited his family doctor. Instead of relief, he was handed a diagnosis he never expected: multiple sclerosis. This immune disorder causes the body to attack its own nervous system, eating away at the protective coating around the nerves. Eventually, the patient's limbs fail to function and even their brain ceases to operate correctly.

Time crept forward and life unfolded as the doctor had warned. While walking down a sidewalk, he would stumble and fall. Standing in an elevator, he'd lose his balance and smash into the wall. Strangers would often assume he was drunk, and Sam was helpless to combat their perceptions. One day he realized things were getting worse quickly when he found himself crawling through the house to get to the bathroom. He was forced to begin using a wheelchair. Today, Sam sometimes has to have help to complete the simplest tasks. He can no longer pick up his legs to step into a bathtub and has to sit in a chair when he showers.

Somehow Sam has avoided growing angry and bitter through it all. When I emailed him to ask how he'd retained his joy, he sent back the following reply:

> I was reading my Bible one day and a passage in
> Scripture jumped off the page. It was so real to me

that I couldn't just casually read past it. The Apostle Paul was talking about how he struggled just like me. He had a "thorn in the flesh" that he had prayed at least three times for God to remove, but to no avail. Of course God told him why. I now realize that MS is not my battle anymore; it's God's. Suddenly, I had an example to look to.

I still may have to deal with the physical limitations, but it's truly not a battle. As Rick Warren has said, "If you want God to bless you and use you greatly, you must be willing to walk with a limp the rest of your life, because God uses weak people." I take his advice literally. Though I am still learning what all this means, one thing I know: when I can't, He can.

There's a reason tough times come and stick around longer than we'd like. Because in your worst misery you experience the best of God—if you look for Him. His arms embrace you in the living room as you sob over your divorce. His hand sits upon your shoulder when you receive the dreaded diagnosis. He walks beside you as you face the misery of your job on Monday mornings. While you wrestle, He draws you into the shadow of His strength.

I love to play golf, and like most golfers I want to see every shot as it leaves the club and track its flight (assuming it has one!). It frustrates me when a good shot gets lost in the sun. I have to helplessly say to my partner, "I never saw it. Where did it go?" My blood pressure rises when they reply, "Beats me. I never saw it either." As I've continued to play, I've learned that overcast days present golfers with optimum playing conditions. You can see the ball cleanly and track its trajectory when gray clouds hide the sunshine.

In this sense, life is a lot like golf. The sunny days are wonderful. But the overcast days allow us to see God most clearly, experience His presence most strongly, and feel His strength most vividly.

Twenty minutes after I gave Big Mike permission to let go, he drifted peacefully into eternity. Each time I drive past his home, I think of all he taught me. That tough times are inevitable, but the way we respond can change everything. That no life is all roses and no thorns, for you cannot have one and not the other. His illness cleared the way for him to make life's greatest decision and to achieve life's greatest victory. It's not an easy truth, but it's a truth nonetheless.

Today, Mike feels no pain and is at peace. The cancer is gone and he rests in the presence of his Maker. So take heart as you face your own tough time. The greater the pain, the deeper the suffering, the harder the situation, the nearer He is and the dearer He will become if you will look and listen for Him. And if you do, He will make sure you see and hear Him.

· ·

Winning Strategy 8:
Stand Under the Shadow of God's Strength.

· ·

Afterword

The Monday Morning Challenge to Remain Standing

"Monday is the key day of the week."

GAELIC PROVERB

Like an antique collector at an estate sale, you've perused the stockpile of God's winning strategies for facing tough times. You now have a trunk full of advice drawn from stories of great men and women who've found victory in difficulty. How and when should you start to implement these principles?

Why not begin this coming Monday morning? Why *this* *Monday?* Because I don't want you to just read this book and walk away from it like we do most books. I want you to begin this coming Monday with a new attitude, ready to attack all the problems that Mondays seem to bring armed with the strategies you have found with this book.

Why Monday? Monday may seem an odd choice. After all, it's perhaps the most disliked day of the week. No other day is vilified, cursed, maligned, dreaded, and even downright feared like Monday. As you can guess, more people call in sick on Mondays than any other day of the week. Think about it: ever heard of a restaurant named TGIM? The Carpenters sang "Rainy Days and Mondays"—not Tuesdays, Wednesdays, or Thursdays— always get us down. Mondays more than any other day tend to knock us down with the challenges of a new week of unknowns: dreaded diagnoses, difficult meetings, unexpected assignments, and personal confrontations put off for the weekend.

I suspect it could be scientifically proved that more frowning, complaining, moaning and groaning, faultfinding, criticizing, bickering, and arguing occurs on Monday than any other day. Adults complain about having to go back to work; kids complain about going back to school; everyone complains that the weekend was just a dream. Yes, Monday is life's wake-up call to the real world. More than any other day, Monday meets us at the door with the gloves on, ready to knock us down.

Go back just three days from Monday. You hear a sigh across the land from early Friday morning to late in the afternoon. It reverberates from metal prisons stuck on freeway off-ramps stretching from Los Angeles to New York. The plaintive sound is heard from cubicles in corporate offices to tiny offices in concrete basements. If sung in unison, it would come from the throats of the largest choir ever assembled. Custodians and CEOs utter the same words always on the same day of the week: "Thank God it's Friday."

This sigh or cry comes from battle-weary waiters, information technologists, computer programmers, schoolteachers (especially schoolteachers), lawyers, accountants, and myriad other professions—even homemakers are not exempt. As Sunday draws to a close, the feeling of dread that "Monday's coming" hits the pit of the stomach. Some call it Black Monday. We know that we're going to wake up with the Monday-morning blues, and like that cold we feel coming on, no medicine can stop it. For so many, each week has become a war of attrition followed by a brief respite before the battle of the real world resumes all over again.

Mourning Monday morning is a universal malady that affects billions of people regardless of where they work. Even people who like their jobs dread Mondays. Unemployed people hate Mondays because it's a painful reminder that they don't have a job and they have to start all over trying to find one. Indeed, for them Mondays are the most difficult times to still stand when so many voices are saying "just give up."

So why am I suggesting that Monday is the perfect time to begin reorienting your life according to these winning strategies? Because even though weekends may be a ceasefire where guns are reloaded and ammunition is restocked, the Monday morning battle often determines the outcome of the war for the rest of the week. Monday is the day when you will determine whether you will remain standing the rest of the week. And the victories you achieve this week will reshape your whole month, and your month will flavor your year, and the outcome of your year can change the course of your life.

Many of the most important decisions of your week occur on Monday mornings:

You decide whether to even go back into the battle of a tough job or quit.

You face the challenge of the first day of a new career.

You begin a new effort to lead a company or department on the brink of collapse back into the black.

You confront the reality of another week living in a marriage speeding toward the cliff of divorce.

You have to face that friend who has stabbed you in the back and determine if you'll let the cancer of bitterness continue to grow.

You snatch up the first appointment of the week with your doctor only to find the tumor was malignant.

On Mondays, character is revealed and built. Winners are separated from losers. The greatest rewards are harvested and the greatest regrets are experienced. In so many ways, whether you're still standing or have thrown in the towel is determined on Monday.

What if you decided to make this coming Monday a pet project for renovating your life? What if you decided this Monday that, whatever happens today, you will still be standing for the rest of the week? What if these key strategies became your field guide for facing this dreadful day? What if this Monday became the model of how you would face *every day*?

Every day, you and I play the game of life. We smack the alarm clock, slurp our coffee, kiss our loved ones good-bye, and set our eyes like a flint. We bear down on the day's demands and "git'r done." But I've found that if I can, for one moment, lift my eyes from the rugged path and look beyond the here and now, I can see a new light, another route. I find that too often I walk through life with my head down, grinding out my existence, and I never really look beyond what's always right in front of me. This is called perspective. And I have to be intentional about keeping it fresh and vibrant.

I'm challenging you to mark your calendar for next Monday morning and decide to make it a day where you'll begin to shift your perspective. Suspend your normal view of the challenges you face. Make a list of ways you'll implement a handful of the winning strategies you've learned, and keep them in your pocket. Let this piece of paper become your pocket-revolver arming you with enough rounds to gain victory over the toughest battles you'll face.

I don't know what challenges you face that want to knock you down for the count. Perhaps it's a crippling disease that makes every day Monday for you. Maybe it's a crumbling marriage, and you find yourself tempted to surrender to that voice telling you to throw in the towel. It could be a job that you despise. Whatever they are, I urge you to take the anxiety and frustration and challenge of that situation and begin to transform it through God's winning strategies that you've found in His Word and in this book.

When life threatens to trip you up, push you over, or knock you down, remember, you aren't the first person to take that punch, face that giant, or stumble over that obstacle, and you won't be the last. But others have stood and are still standing, and by God's grace and through His power, you can too. The One who still stands after dying on a cross is standing with you today—and that knowledge is the greatest place of all to stand!

So my prayer for you as you suit up the armor, put on the helmet, and strap on your sword to go out to the battles of life that we all face is that at the end of the day when you have taken the best shots the enemy has, you will, by God's grace, be still standing!

Notes

Chapter 1: When Life Knocks You Down
1. Psalm 56:9 ESV.
2. John 16:33.

Chapter 2: When Life Is Physically Draining
1. "Facts on Stress," *Washington Post*, January 23, 2007.
2. www.Stressdirections.com/personal/about_stress.
3. Exodus 18:13-18.
4. Exodus 18:19-23.
5. Exodus 18:19.
6. John 17:4 ESV.

Chapter 3: When Life Is Dragging You Down
1. This was a different church from the one I talk about in chapter 1.
2. "Major Depressive Disorder Among Adults," National Institute of Mental Health, www.nimh.nih.gov/statistics/1MDD_ADULT.shtml.
3. "National Health Priority Areas Mental Health: A Report Focusing on Depression," Australian Institute of Health and Welfare, 1998. Depression statistics in Australia are comparable to those of the U.S. and U.K.
4. Mental Health America (formerly National Mental Health Association) study reported in *MSNBC Health Today,* March 10, 2004.
5. "National Healthcare Quality Report 2003," Agency for Healthcare Research and Quality (AHRQ). www.ahrq.gov/qual/measurix.htm.
6. *Psychology Today*, October 1988.
7. 1 Kings 19:1-2.
8. 1 Kings 19:3-5.
9. Exodus 3.
10. Numbers 22:21-33.
11. *Psychology Today*, October 1988.
12. Bob Russell, *Jesus Lord of Your Personality* (West Monroe, LA: Howard Publishing, 2002), 103-4.
13. Henri Nouwen, *Can You Drink the Cup?* (Notre Dame, IN: Ave Maria Press, 2006), 64-65.
14. 1 Peter 1:8.
15. 1 Kings 19:5-6.

16. 1 Kings 19:4.
17. 1 Kings 19: 9-10.
18. 1 Kings 19:11-12.
19. 1 Kings 19:15-16.

Chapter 4: When Life Is Unfair
1. Nancy Gibbs, "One Day in America," *Time,* November 15, 2007.
2. Genesis 1:16.
3. Genesis 37:2.
4. Adapted from Max Lucado, *Cast of Characters* (Nashville, TN: Thomas Nelson, 2008), 125.
5. Genesis 37:23-28.
6. Genesis 39:1.
7. Genesis 39:2.
8. Genesis 39:6-10.
9. Genesis 39:19-20.
10. Genesis 39:21.
11. Genesis 41:39-43.
12. Genesis 39:2-4.
13. http://truthspeaker.wordpress.com/2011/02/03/david-and-svea-flood/. This story is based on the book *Aggie: The Inspiring Story of a Girl Without a Country* (previously published under the title *One Witness*) by Aggie Hurst.

Chapter 5: When Life Seems Impossible
1. Cited by Alister E. McGrath, *Intellectuals Don't Need God and Other Modern Myths* (Grand Rapids, MI: Zondervan, 1993), 15.
2. Genesis 17:1-8.
3. Joshua 1:1-2.
4. Joshua 1:5.
5. Psalm 50:10.
6. John 15:5.
7. Luke 12:21.
8. Mark 8:36.
9. Joshua 1:8.
10. See for example, http://askville.amazon.com/Americans-read-Bible-Daily-Basis/AnswerViewer.do?requestId=11803750.
11. Proverbs 17:28.
12. Joshua 1:6.
13. Joshua 1:5.

Chapter 6: When Life Tempts You to Sell Out

1. Daniel 1:1-2.
2. Daniel 1:3-4.
3. Daniel 1:5-7.
4. Daniel 1:8.
5. 1 Corinthians 4:4.
6. Acts 24:16.
7. Daniel 1:9.
8. Deuteronomy 6:5.
9. Psalm 119:11.
10. 1 Samuel 2:30.

Chapter 7: When Life Says "Run"

1. John Maxwell, *The 21 Irrefutable Laws of Leadership* (Nashville, TN: Thomas Nelson Publishers, 1998), 199.
2. See Esther 2:7.
3. Esther 3:1-2.
4. Esther 3:5-6.
5. Compare Exodus 17:8-16; 1 Samuel 15:1-33; Esther 3:1.
6. Esther 3:8-12.
7. Esther 3:13-14.
8. Esther 4:11.
9. Esther 4:13-14.
10. C.J. Mahaney, *The Cross-Centered Life* (Sisters, OR: Multnomah Publishers, 2002), 54.
11. Esther 6:10-14.

Chapter 8: When Life Seems to Be Against You

1. Nehemiah 6:1-2.
2. Proverbs 14:23.
3. Nehemiah 6:4.
4. Nehemiah 6:3.
5. Nehemiah 6:5-7.
6. Charles R. Swindoll, *Laugh Again* (Nashville, TN: Thomas Nelson Publishers, 1992), 230.
7. Nehemiah 6:8.
8. Nehemiah 6:9.
9. Nehemiah 6:10.
10. Nehemiah 6:11.

11. Cited by Dennis Rainey, *One Home at a Time* (Carol Stream, IL: Tyndale House Publishers, 1999), 178.

12. Nehemiah 6:15.

Chapter 9: When Life Is Insufferable

1. 2 Corinthians 12:7 esv.

2. Psalm 68:19 nkjv.

3. 2 Corinthians 12:8.

4. 2 Corinthians 12:9.

5. 2 Corinthians 12:9-10.

6. Ron Dunn, *When Heaven Is Silent* (Nashville, TN: Thomas Nelson Publishers, 1994), 217.

Acknowledgments

As always, many people besides the author are responsible for a book. Without their help, a book fails to materialize or reach its full potential. I'd like to thank a few of them here:

First, I thank Bob Hawkins, a man whose middle name is "integrity." He has become a trusted friend whose partnership has been one tremendous blessing. Thanks for the honor of partnering with you and the Harvest House team on this project.

Thanks to Rod Morris, an editor who takes his craft seriously. You make writers believe you care about their books as if they were your own. You are a joy to work with and your editorial polish puts a real shine on each manuscript you touch.

To Robert and Erik Wolgemuth, my literary agents. It is a pleasure to be represented by your firm, and you are both class acts.

To Tim Willard, I offer my appreciation for the insights, additions, and tweaks that make this book more readable and enjoyable.

To my sons James, Joshua, and daughter-in-love Natalie. We stand together as family. And to Harper and Presley, my amazing grandchildren. I pray you will face tough times with faith and not fear, knowing God is with you and the battle is His.

To Jonathan, my beloved middle son, whose belief in me has blessed me beyond measure. I wouldn't be writing these words without your encouragement and help.

To Teresa, my precious wife, best friend, and soul mate. You've helped me stand tall for thirty-six years. I love you more than ever.

Finally, all glory and praise to my Lord and Savior Jesus Christ, whose victorious Sunday morning resurrection allows me to face each difficult Monday with confidence. There is nobody like Jesus!

About the Author

James Merritt (@drjamesmerritt) is lead pastor of Cross Pointe Church in Duluth, Georgia, and host of *Touching Lives*, an internationally broadcast television show airing weekly in all 50 states and 122 countries. He has written seven books including, *How to Impact and Influence Others* and *God, I've Got a Question*. As a respected religious leader, James has been interviewed by media outlets including *60 Minutes, The New York Times, ABC World News Tonight, Time Magazine,* and *Hannity and Colmes.*

From 2000 to 2002, James served as president for the largest Protestant denomination in America, the Southern Baptist Convention. He earned his bachelor's degree from Stetson University and his master of divinity degree and doctor of philosophy degree from the Southern Baptist Theological Seminary in Louisville, Kentucky. His heart for pastors has also resulted in PastorsEdge.com, a popular leadership resource for ministers.

James and his wife, Teresa, have been married for more than thirty-five years. They have three sons and two grandchildren.

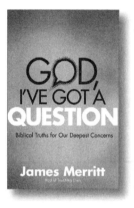

Other Books by James Merritt

God, I've Got a Question
Biblical Truth for Our
Deepest Concerns

James Merritt, popular pastor, author, and host of the television show *Touching Lives,* knows that when people wrestle with doubts, they are missing out on the security, promises, and power of Christ.

Avoiding academic lingo, Merritt presents relatable, relevant responses to the hard questions that seekers and Christians hesitate to ask or answer:

- Why is there so much suffering in the world if God is in control?

- How can I discover God's will for my life?

- Why is Jesus the only way to God, and how can I defend this?

- What should I do about the moral gray areas of my life?

- Why should anybody believe the Bible?

Whether read straight through or used as a reference for specific topics, this insightful resource reveals the uncompromised truths of the Christian faith and the depth and importance of its precepts for every person, every life.

How to Impact and Influence Others
9 Keys to Successful Leadership

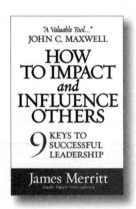

A person's character—who he is—determines the impact he has on others. James Merritt, senior pastor of Cross Pointe Church and host of the television program *Touching Lives*, unlocks nine key character qualities that, if consistently exercised and seen by others, will influence them to reach their full potential.

Readers of this book will be motivated to leave a lasting impact in a number of ways, such as

- making sure someone sees, hears, or feels love from them each day
- letting God's joy shine through their life
- being kind to someone every day
- being faithful and dependable
- treating others as more important

No one can do anything about his heritage, but he can do something about his legacy. Beginning today, he can become the kind of person who makes a life-changing difference for others, perhaps even an *eternal* difference. *How to Impact and Influence Others* shows the way to a life of surpassing influence.